DEEP FOUNDATIONS WORKBOOK TEACHERS EDITION

{RICK PETERMAN}

ISBN: 978-0-9883419-5-

Copyright 2020

I0172510

This workbook is complete with informative answers and additional information which acts as an elaboration to the book Deep Foundations.

Textbook Photo & Web-page Link

https://www.amazon.com/DEEP-FOUNDATIONS-Biblical-Present-Future-ebook-dp-B01NBPM0QF/dp/B01NBPM0QF

I believe the information contained in this book will be interesting, relevant, and useful to at least four types of people.

To the Skeptic:
The honest doubter can see how the Bible has logical and reasonable answers to the problems in our world. It reveals the causes and effects we see all around us, as well as the reasonable conclusions, we often don't see in time. (Galatians 6:7)

To the Truth Seeker:
You may be looking at all the different religions of the world with their isolated and disconnected ideas that promote contradictions. It is important to know how to test them to find out if they have true lasting treasure or are just an illusion that temporarily makes you feel good. (John 8:32)

To the Believer:
It gives a foundation for our belief, connecting the facts between the origins of Genesis 1 to the destiny of Revelation 22. By examining the details and illustrating the sequences of events, we can see and understand how redemption works, as well as the many benefits available to us. (Luke 6:48)

To the Spiritual Leader:
It encourages and challenges us with truth, exposing the Deceivers' strategy. It gives Biblical insight to the mysteries and questions of life. It helps us to envision our future rewards, reflect on our present position, and take a closer look at our past traditions and assumptions in the light of our ultimate authority, the Word of God. (2 Timothy 2:7)

A Biblical Tour of Our Past, Present & Future

DEEP FOUNDATIONS

Rick Peterman

CONCORDANCE

Section 1 – Identification

Section 2 – Illustration

Section 3 – Application

Section 4 – Transformation

Section 5 – Illumination

Workbook Introduction

Psalm 11:3

If the foundations be destroyed, what can the righteous do?

We need to learn, trust and apply God's Word. God's Word is the foundation that cannot be destroyed (1-Peter 1:23-25). If we build on any other foundation than God's Word, then it will be shaken and destroyed (1-Corinthians 3:11-15). To establish an indestructible foundation to support a blessed life we need knowledge of God's Word (Psalm 119:104-105). Then we need to build on that foundation (Luke 6:47:48). The importance of knowledge is mentioned 7 times in the 3 short chapters of 2-Peter.

As in the example question and answer above, write an answer in your own words for each question on a separate paper or electronic device and be sure to number your answers to match the questions. Some answers may be long and others just a word or two. Most of the answers are found in the Bible. Therefore, try to think of a biblical reference to support your answer and possibly include it in your answer. The book Deep Foundations will help us to see the historic context and proper interpretations to understand the biblical answers to these important questions. Therefore, it is important that every teacher read the book Deep Foundations before using this workbook to teach a class. By doing this, you will see the big picture and realize how answering each question in order is building a stronger foundation to support a consistent understanding of God's Word.

I have copied a selection of verses from the King James Bible (Mark 4:21-25, Ezekiel 12:1-2, Isaiah 42:6-7, Acts 26:18, Matthew 5:14-19, Ephesians 5:8-17, 2-Corinthians 4:1-7) and placed them here for you to read. This is like a three-way conversation between the Holy Spirit, Jesus, and His disciples. We are considered His disciple if we are dedicated to Jesus. Reading these verses is like listening in to the Holy Spirit talking to the disciples, then the Holy Spirit talking to Jesus at the beginning of His earthly ministry, then Jesus talking to His disciples, and their response. Some people underestimate the importance of the Holy Spirit. If we do not receive the Holy Spirit of Jesus in our heart we cannot be saved (Romans 8:9). It is the Holy Spirit that makes the Word of God come alive to us (John 14:26). Lets ask the Holy Spirit to illuminate God's Word to us as we read the following verses.

(Holy Spirit talking to the disciples) **And He said unto them, Is a candle brought to be put under a bushel, or under a bed? and not to be set on a candlestick? For there is nothing hid, which shall not be manifested; neither was any thing kept secret, but that it should come abroad. If any man have ears to hear, let him hear. And He said unto them, Take heed what ye hear: with what measure ye mete, it shall be measured to you: and unto you that hear shall more be given. For he that hath, to him shall be given: and he that hath not, from him shall be taken even that which he hath. The Word of the LORD also came unto me,** *(Holy Spirit talking to Jesus)* **saying, son of man, thou dwellest in the midst of a rebellious house, which have eyes to see, and see not; they have ears to hear, and hear not: for they are a rebellious house. I the LORD have called thee in righteousness, and will hold thine hand, and will keep thee, and give thee for a covenant of the people, for a light of the Gentiles; To open the blind eyes, to bring out the prisoners from the prison, and them that sit in darkness out of the prison house. To open their eyes, and to turn them from darkness to light, and from the power of Satan unto God, that they may receive forgiveness of sins, and inheritance among them which are sanctified by faith that is in Me.** *(Jesus talking to His disciples)* **Ye are the light of the world. A city that is set on an hill cannot be hid. Neither do men light a candle, and put it under a bushel, but on a candlestick; and it giveth light unto all that are in the house. Let your light so shine before men, that they may see your good works, and glorify your Father which is in heaven. Think not that I am come to destroy the law, or the prophets: I am not come to destroy, but to fulfil. For verily I say unto you, Till heaven and earth pass, one jot or one tittle shall in no wise pass from the law, till all be fulfilled. Whosoever therefore shall break one of these least**

commandments, and shall teach men so, he shall be called the least in the kingdom of heaven: but whosoever shall do and teach them, the same shall be called great in the kingdom of heaven. For ye were sometimes darkness, but now are ye light in the Lord: walk as children of light: (For the fruit of the Spirit is in all goodness and righteousness and truth;) Proving what is acceptable unto the Lord. And have no fellowship with the unfruitful works of darkness, but rather reprove them. For it is a shame even to speak of those things which are done of them in secret. But all things that are reproved are made manifest by the light: for whatsoever doth make manifest is light. Wherefore He saith, Awake thou that sleepest, and arise from the dead, and Christ shall give thee light. See then that ye walk circumspectly, not as fools, but as wise, redeeming the time, because the days are evil. Wherefore be ye not unwise, but understanding what the will of the Lord is. *(the disciples response to Jesus and the Holy Spirit)* **Therefore seeing we have this ministry, as we have received mercy, we faint not; But have renounced the hidden things of dishonesty, not walking in craftiness, nor handling the Word of God deceitfully; but by manifestation of the truth commending ourselves to every man's conscience in the sight of God. But if our gospel be hid, it is hid to them that are lost: In whom the god of this world hath blinded the minds of them which believe not, lest the light of the glorious gospel of Christ, who is the image of God, should shine unto them. For we preach not ourselves, but Christ Jesus the Lord; and ourselves your servants for Jesus' sake. For God, who commanded the light to shine out of darkness, hath shined in our hearts, to give the light of the knowledge of the glory of God in the face of Jesus Christ. But we have this treasure in earthen vessels, that the excellency of the power may be of God, and not of us.** *(This ends this quote directly from God's Word).*

You can simply use this book and read the questions and answers for your own personal Bible study or use this book to start a Bible study class. If you want to use this book to start a class in a Christian school or college and have the time and desire to be more thorough, I believe it is best to start the classes by reading the textbook *Deep Foundations* one chapter at a time. Some students have trouble comprehending what they read. Therefore, I believe reading *Deep Foundations* audibly will be beneficial. At the conclusion of each chapter, read the workbook questions for that chapter and have the students write down their answers or discuss them one question at a time. Feel free to let God lead you in your class process and biblical discussions. Some questions may take the whole time allotted for the class to clearly answer and others just a few minutes. The answers in this workbook are provided to help you conclude the discussions with factual answers and biblical references. You can read the answers from the workbook and look up the verses, but feel free to improvise. Let God lead you as to how you use these answers. A few sentences in the student edition have missing words indicated by underlined question marks *?????*. This edition has the question marks replaced by the correct word. There are optional questions at the end of each chapter, which are a matter of your personal opinion. If you choose to include them, you can prepare a short answer of what you think and why you feel that way. You can also use this workbook to do smaller classes on specific subjects by just focusing on the chapters pertaining to that subject. For example, if you wanted to do a class on prophecy you should read chapter 6 and section 4 in the book *Deep Foundations* and then do the questions and answers for those chapters from this workbook. Or at Christmas time you could do a class on the birth of Christ and just focus on chapter 5, or at Easter you could focus on chapters 9,10, and 11.

Preamble

₁) What year did it become possible to have a standard as to how to spell a word and why?

1828, that is when Webster's dictionary was published. Before that there was no standard or authority on how to spell a word. For instance the word privately is spelled privily in Matthew 1:19, Matthew 2:7 and in thirteen other verses throughout the King James Bible. That was fine in 1611 when the first edition of King James became available because Webster did not complete his dictionary until 1828. Therefore, for more than 200 years after the King James Bible was written, there was no standard to verify the *correct spelling of a word. Another example of a spelling issue that predates the King James Bible is the William Tyndale New Testament, written in 1534. I have copied Matthew 3:2 for you to see; "**saynge; Repet the kyngdome of heue is at honde.**" As bad as this spelling is, it was not wrong until 1828.*

₂₎ Is it important to have a standard to verify accuracy and why?

Yes, otherwise everything becomes a matter of opinion, which is where we get into situational ethics (Judges 17:6, Judges 21:25). Judges 17 starts with a thief buying a preacher. This confused man employed a preacher to tell him what he wanted to hear. Judges 21 ends with family breakdown, immorality and unimaginable violence. Popularity may make a standard that unites people, but it does not verify truth (2-Timothy 4:3-4). I have heard many people use these verses in 2 Timothy as a standard for Christ return. This behavior is not new, nor is it the standard that God uses for Christ return. If we read the context of 2-Timothy 4:3-4 we will see the point of the passage is that God wants us to focus on what is true, not on what is popular (2-Timothy 4:1-8).

₃₎ What is the best standard to verify truth in spiritual things such as life after death?

God's Written Word is the standard to verify truth (John 17:17). God's Word is permanent, opposing opinions are temporary (Isaiah 40:8). The Bible reveals that there is life after death (Romans 6:23), and it is a free gift to those that come through Jesus.

₄₎ Does the standard overrule conflicting opinions?

Yes - the standard is the ruler to measure accuracy (Psalm 33:10-11). Every opinion that stands against God's Word will be proven wrong sooner or latter (1-Peter 1:24-25, Ephesians 4:14). What about non-christian people who came back from the dead and claim they have seen Heaven? Temporary euphoric out-of-body experiences can be a deceptive temptation from the Devil (Luke 4:5-8) to make you think you don't need to follow God's Word to enter glory. Satan, the angel of light can seduce some individuals with a temporary heavenly experience through drugs or death (temporarily clinically dead), but only God can give you eternal life in Heaven. Those preaching or believing in a false gospel will not be blessed by God in the end. The gospel is God's plan for salvation. It tells us how to receive eternal life, which qualifies us for Heaven. The Apostle Paul affirmed the importance of the biblical gospel (Galatians 1:8-12, 2-Timothy 2:15).

CHAPTER 1
RECEIVING TRUTH OR BLINDING DECEPTIONS

5} What is a simple definition of the Hebrew word Selah?

Pause and think about that

6} What is a simple definition of meditation?

Meditation is taking time to think about and focus on specific information. During meditation we organize our thoughts so we can see all the ramifications of the information.

7} Who is the author of the Holy Bible?

God - 2-Timothy 3:16, God used His chosen people to act as His secretaries to record His Word. God used a variety of different godly men as instruments, just as an author might use different pens or fonts, each having its own color or style.

8} Is God able to preserve His written word, which we call the Bible?

Yes - Mark 13:31, 1-Peter 1:23-25, Psalm 12:6-7. This question is the foundation of the division and debate over biblical manuscripts. There are people that spend years studying this subject that strongly disagree with each other. Therefore in a class you may want to just share what the Bible states on the matter and trust God to preserve and reveal His Word. Then move on to the following questions. I share the following information not as an expert, but to acknowledge the commonly accepted facts regarding the history of the Greek manuscripts used to produce English Bibles.

Since the 1800s we've had 2 different lines of Greek manuscripts from which Bibles are translated.

One is called the Preserved Line, Traditional Text or Textus Receptus. These are the manuscripts from which the King James Version (KJ) and the Modern English Bible (MEV) are translated from. These are the manuscripts used by William Tyndale and Martin Luther as a foundation for the Reformation and the Great Awakening of the 1500s. These were the manuscripts uses to bring us out of the dark ages and form the English Bible Based Church.

The popular NIV, NASB, NLT, as well as most of the modern Bibles are translated from a different line of manuscripts. The other line of manuscripts are often referred to as the Revised text or the Alexandrian line. These are the manuscripts Westcott and Hort reconstruct to produce their Greek text of 1881. Both of these Greek scholars rejected the Textus Receptus. It appears they were looking for truth in some of the wrong places. In collage they were members of the Ghostly Guild (a group that investigated spiritual phenomena and seances). Darwin publish his book in 1859 which Hort admitted influenced his belief about creation. He was also uncommitted to the infallibility of Scripture and doubted a literal eternal Hell. None of us are perfect but these things should make us hesitate about appointing them as the final authority on the Word of God.

After considering these things, the bottom line is how do these manuscripts differ?

In Westcott and Hort's Greek text of 1881 many times the difference is just subtle word changes that are less pointed or put a slightly different spin on the sentence. Other times a word is removed completely. For example in 2-Peter 1:21 the word "holy" is remove.

2-Peter 1:21

21) For the prophecy came not in old time by the will of man: but **holy** men of God spake as they were moved by the Holy Ghost(KJV).

*21) For no prophecy at any time was produced by the will of man, but **holy** men moved by the Holy Spirit spoke from God(MEV).*

21) For prophecy never had its origin in the human will, but prophets, though human, spoke from God as they were carried along by the Holy Spirit(NIV).

21) for no prophecy was ever made by an act of human will, but men moved by the Holy Spirit spoke from God(NAS).

The definition of the word HOLY is that someone or something is set apart and dedicated unto God. This is a word of clarity that not everyone would qualify to bring forth God's Word.

Westcott and Hort's Greek text of 1881 not only left out words, they also left out whole sentences. For instance they leave out Acts 8:37 which acknowledges the Biblical order of water baptism is after salvation. They also leave out Matthew 17:21 about spiritual warfare. In 1-John 5:7 they removed the clear references to the trinity of God.

There is a lot of debate about the ending of Mark. There are actually 4 different endings for the Book of Mark. Two of the oldest manuscripts do not have Mark 16:9-20. They are also missing other portions of scripture. Two other manuscripts add things and are commonly dismissed as coming from corrupted ancient manuscripts. This proves that there are a few manuscripts that were tampered with and therefore corrupted. This should not surprise us, because without God's help people make mistakes. Also the Devil has a long history of changing, replacing, twisting and denying God's Word. The Devil was not born yesterday. The Deceiver often plants deceptions, corruptions and delusions that he intends to use latter to confuse and destroy people. Since Satan cannot destroy God's Word, his common practice is to surround it with counterfeits and confusion (1-John 4:1, Matthew 7:15-16,20, Genesis 3:1-5). Regarding Mark's ending, Mark 16:9-20 agrees and supports the other Gospel writers. There are 1,653 Greek manuscripts that include Mark 16:9-20. Some of them are damaged, but show that they had the whole passage when they were pristine. This means that 99.8% of the Greek manuscripts available include Mark 16:9-20. One final though regarding the claim that the two oldest manuscripts are the most accurate. It would be naive to assume the NIV published in 1973 is more accurate than the MEV published in 2014, just because it is older. They were produced by different people for different purposes at different places. The same is true about the different manuscript lines. Many question why Mark 16:9 starts over to tell the events of resurrection day from the beginning. That is peculiar but one reason for this is covered in the book Deep Foundations at the beginning of chapter 10-Resurrection Day.

9} Will the Holy Bible ever cease to exist?

No - Luke 21:33

10} Is the Holy Bible less true if it contradicts many or any of our popular beliefs?

No - Isaiah 40:8

11} Are we deceived if we believe a lie?

Yes – Ephesians 4:14, Deuteronomy 11:16, 1-Corinthians 15:33-34

12} Is every translation of the Bible 100% accurate?

No, There are some translations that are more accurate than others. Most modern translations mistranslate Exodus 12:40 which then contradicts Galatians 3:17. The KJ, NKJ and the MEV use the word sojourning which means to make camp in the medial of a journey. How this make a big difference to many things including history and prophecy is detailed in Deep Foundations chapters 1 and 6. Now lets look at the difference in the wording of Isaiah 14:12 between the NIV and the KJ.

Isaiah 14:12 KJ

How art thou fallen from heaven, O <u>Lucifer</u>, son of the morning! how art thou cut down to the ground, which didst weaken the nations!

Isaiah 14:12 NIV

How you have fallen from heaven, <u>morning star</u>, son of the dawn! You have been cast down to the earth, you who once laid low the nations!

The name Lucifer means light bearer and is a well-recognized name for Satan. For KJ accuracy the MEV Bible is a great modern translation. For example, the MEV uses the name Lucifer, but many other modern translations call Lucifer a bright star or morning star. The problem with calling Lucifer the "Morning Star" is that in every translation Jesus said He was the "Morning Star" Revelation 22:16, Revelation 2:28. Mistranslations add to the confusion and fuel skepticism about what the Bible says. Mistranslations and misguided traditions encourage people to believe things that don't add up. For instance let's look at John 19:14 and Mark 15:25. John uses our gentile clock so this verse and others verify Christ's trial was at 6:00 in the morning, not at noon (as stated in the NIV). Mark uses the Jewish clock and records that they crucified Jesus at the 3rd hour of the day which was 9 AM on our clock.

*Both the Modern English Version and the King James are very accurate translations. The MEV is a modern translation that is easy to read but the King James is more consistent in its uses of words like **soul**, **repent** and **Hell** which gives us a better understanding of these words. For that reason I consider the KJ to be the best study Bible & the MEV the best reading Bible.*

King James was translated from the Greek and Hebrew but in reality the KJ New testament is actually 93% Tyndale Bible. The 47 translators couldn't improve on Tyndale's wording. The history of the KJ Bible begins with William Tyndale at the time of the Reformation. William Tyndale was a genius when it came to languages and felt called of God to translate from the original Greek and Hebrew into an English Bible. During Tyndale's life it was illegal to wright or quote the Bible in English. Latin was the only biblical language in England. In 1519 people were burned at the stake for teaching children the Lords prayer & the 10 Commandments in English. 4 years latter in 1523 William Tyndale asked the church's permission to print an English Bible. He was denied and left the country. He went to Germany where they had more printing presses and he could hide from the English church authority. William Tyndale printed his 1st English Bible in 1526 and revised it in 1534. These Bibles were the 1st Bibles that were translated from the Greek and Hebrew to English. Tyndale was tracked down brought to England and Martyred 1536 for printing an English Bible. They tied him to a post to be burned at the stake. Because he was a priest before they lit the fire they strangled him. His last words were "Lord open the King's eyes." 2 years latter in 1538 William Tyndale's prayer was answered. The heart of King Henry the 8th was changed and he decreed that every English church would have an English Bible to read.

The Roots of the King James Bible goes back to an announced servant of God named William Tyndale who became a martyr during the time of a Great Awakening we call the Reformation. It was the beginning of a Bible based church.

Here are a few popular quotes directly from the Tyndale Bible

"Ask and it shall be given you, seek, and ye shall find; knock, and it shall be opened unto you *(Matthew 7)*

With God all things are possible *(Matthew 19)*

In him we live and move and have our being *(Acts 17)*

Behold, I stand at the door and knock *(Revelation 3)*

Am I my brother's keeper? *(Genesis 4)*

The salt of the earth *(Matthew 5)*

Where two or three are gathered together *(Matthew 18)*

They made light of it *(Matthew 22)*

The spirit is willing but the flesh is week *(Matthew 26)*

Eat, drink, and be marry *(Luke 12)*

A law unto themselves *(Romans 2)*

The powers that be *(Romans 13)*

The patience of Job *(James 5)*

the just shall live by faith *(Romans 1, Galatians 3, and Hebrews 10)"*

The King James does mistranslate a word from Jesus in Matthew 12:40. The definition of the Greek word in that aria is "huge fish with a big gaping mouth," but the KJ uses the word "whale." This contradicts Jonah 1:17. In defense of the 47 King James translators in 1611 and William Tyndale in 1526 they thought whales were fish. It wasn't until December 29 1818 that it was proven in a New York courtroom that whales were not fish, but many people continued to call them fish for many years.

These misunderstandings by the translators create confusion and do not reflect God's Word in those arias. If we understand the limitations of the translation, there are still many benefits to reading different translations.

13) **Can Satan appear to be a good angel of light?**

Yes - 2-Corinthians 11:14

14) **What is Satan's most common way to hide the light of God's gems of Truth?**

Satan surrounds the diamond of God's Word with cheap glass and plastic. Satan's many counterfeits, deceptions and ½ truths are easy to find. Popularity does not verify truth or validate a ministry. God may bless you with a large and popular ministry, but popularity does not necessarily verify your ministry. God wants us to be fruitful, but more importantly God wants us to be faithful. Jeremiah was called to an unpopular ministry (Jeremiah 1:9-10, Jeremiah 26:2-8, Jeremiah 29:8-13, Jeremiah 33:1-3). In the end he was vindicated and all the popular false prophets that came against him was put to shame. God's eternal truth is like a pearl of great price (Matthew 13:45-46); it is often hidden (Matthew 13:44) or outnumbered by Satan's temporary distractions. To enjoy the benefits of God's treasures of truth, we need to consider them more valuable than all other opinions, including our own. In every aria our opinions need to become grounded in God's Word and reflect God's ways.

15) Can Satan deceive a Christian leader?

Yes (Matthew 16:23). Particularly if they have been indoctrinated in unbiblical concepts (Mark 7:7-9, Titus 1:14, 2 Timothy 4:2-4) or turn away from God's Word (Galatians 5:1).

16) If we find we have been deceived and are out of harmony with God's Word, what should we do?

Repent, and ask for wisdom to properly apply and live by the truth (Proverbs 3:5-7). You may find it beneficial to meditate on Ephesians 6:10-18. Notice that in Ephesians 6:16 that the truth is the first part of the armor of God that we are to put on. We need to apply the belt of truth to be effective for God and protected from the deceiver. The belt of true is like a belt of light that enables us to see both good and bad things so we can make better choices (Psalms 119:104-105). If we walk in the light of true, it will continue to increase so we can see more things more clearly (Proverbs 4:18-19, Luke 19:26). We need to focus on applying what the light of truth is revealing to us, because if we reject the belt of truth our heart will be darkened (Romans 1:21-22, Matthew 13:12, Matthew 25:29). If our heart becomes contaminated with deceptive darkness we cannot apply the breastplate of righteousness, which enables us to walking in the peace that surpasses understanding (Philippians 4:7-8).

17) Since no one is perfect, as Christians what are the 2 main attitudes we should have toward others?

Love and respect; our motivation should be to help and encourage everyone to do right. I've heard it said that people might not remember what you said, but they will remember how you made them feel. Jesus wants us to treat everyone with love and respect, even in conflict or when correcting or instructing them (Matthew 5:43-47, 1-Timothy 5:1-3).

18) Was the children of Israel slaves in Egypt for 430 years, or 400 years, or less than 150 years?

They were slaves in Egypt less than 150 years. The Genesis genealogy record is a calendar that starts at Adam's creation (Genesis 5:1-3) and ends at Joseph's death (Genesis 50:26). It is important to remember (especially when dating Abraham's birth) that the Genesis genealogy record tracks the bloodline not the firstborn. Israel's slavery started after Joseph died which was long after Abraham died. According to the Genesis genealogy records, there are 215 years between the promise given to Abraham (Genesis 12:1-4) and Jacob going to Egypt (Genesis 47:7-9). Joseph was second in command of Egypt and blessed Israel until Joseph died, 71 years after his reunion with his father (Genesis 50:26). Israel's slavery started after Joseph was dead and forgotten (Exodus 1:6-11) and ended when Moses led them out of Egypt (Exodus 12:40-41 KJV). There is 144 years between Joseph's death and the Passover, but Israel's slavery did not start at Joseph's death. Israel's slavery started after there was "a new king over Egypt, which knew not Joseph." If you can keep these things in mind and answer the next question correctly you will see the conclusive biblical proof that Israel was slaves in Egypt less than 150 years.

19) **How many years does the Bible say there was between Abraham's covenant with God and Moses receiving the 10 commandments?**

*430 years (Galatians 3:17-18). The year Moses lead Israel out of Egypt was the same year he was at Mount Sinai and received the 10 commandments. I believe the promise in Genesis 12:1-4 happened around Abraham's 75th birthday and the confirming covenant in Genesis 15:18 was near the end of that same year. Even if it was the following year, it doesn't change the 430-year span between the Covenant of Promise and the Law of Moses. The book Deep Foundations reveals how the year of the Abrahamic covenant was a **mirror image** of the year Isaac was born. Both years **began** with a **promise**. Both of these covenant years clearly record Abraham's age. The one when Abraham was **75 ending** with a **covenant**, the other when Abraham **turned 100 started** with a **covenant** (circumcision). In the first covenant year time-frame Sodom was **plundered** in the second covenant year time-frame Sodom was **destroyed**. Also, Abraham lacked faith and **lied**, calling Sarah his sister in both covenant years. In both covenant years Sarah needed to be **rescued** by God from a foreign **king**. The first covenant year **began** with seeing the **promise land**. The second covenant year **ended** with seeing the **promise child**,*

*The Bible emphasizes it was **430** years to the **very day** between Abraham's 2-day covenant with God, found in the fifteenth chapter of Genesis and the 2-day feast of Passover and Unleavened Bread (Exodus 12:41). The Passover celebrates freedom from slavery. The feast of Unleavened Bread celebrates Israel's departure from Egypt. The original Passover was on the 430th anniversary of the covenant between God and Abraham. Israel went to Egypt in the middle of that 430-year span (215 years after the covenant). Israel spent the last ½ of those 430 years in Egypt, which is 215-years. For more than 7 decades of those last 215 years Israel enjoyed the best of what Egypt had to offer (Genesis 47:5-6) before they ended up as slaves. These things may seem insignificant but they contain the keys to understanding prophesies about the last generation. These things also reveal how God's predestination and man's free will, work together. When you read chapter 6 of the book Deep Foundations and study the time-chart at the end of the chapter you will see these things clearly.*

Before leaving these 2 questions I decided to add some additional information to help you see the importance and the reality of God's calendar. You may decide not to share the following info with your class, but I wanted you to know the numbers referred to in the previous questions and in chapter 6 do add up correctly and are in complete harmony with the entire Bible. When we get to chapter 6 the false assumptions regarding these numbers and many other false assumptions will be addressed. With that in mind lets look closer at the importance and the accuracy of God's genealogical calendar.

*A good farmer knows the difference between summer and winter (Genesis 8:22). Weather is seasonal, although it can be unusual. I have seen it snow in Fort Lauderdale Florida when I was there in 1977. I personally know Michigan's weather and was snowed in for days during the blizzard of 1978. If I were in Michigan and some forecaster told me in July to get ready for a blizzard tomorrow, I would not be concerned, because July is not the season for blizzards in Michigan. Even if I saw big black storm clouds rolling in, I would not be preparing for a blizzard, nor would I tell others to prepare for a blizzard. What I might do is to prepare for the rain. Just as there are seasons for weather, there are seasons for fulfilled prophecies. **Similar signs can result in***

different events because of the season. *The Bible contains God's calendar, which confirms the prophetic season we are in. In preparation for understanding God's seasons of prophecy, let's first understand God's calendar of historic events.*

If you read the begot calendar in Genesis and number the dates, you will be at 1948 when you come to Genesis 11:26. This is where it gets a little confusing. It would appear that Abraham was born in 1948 but he was not. Terah's 1ˢᵗ born was in 1948 but Abraham was not the 1ˢᵗ born. Abraham was born 60 years latter in 2008.

How do I know that? Look at Gen 12:4 and we see that Abraham was 75 years old when he left Harran. Abraham's journey to the Promise Land started many weeks before this event. Abraham's journey to Canaan started when he was at home in Ur (Nehemiah 9:7, Genesis 15:7). If Abraham was heading for Canaan, then why did Abraham stop and dwell in Harran? Abraham stopped in Harran because he was following his father (Genesis 11:31). What happened in Harran? Abraham's father died (Gen 11:32). What did God tell Abraham to comfort him after His father's death? God promised to make him the head of a great nation (Genesis 12:1-3). Why did Abraham leave Harran? Abraham left Harran at God's direction (Genesis 12:4). How old was Abraham when he left Harran? Abraham was 75 when he left Harran. God did not divide the Bible into chapters, so originally the 5 verses regarding events in Harran were together to tell 1 story. God gave us the specific numbers recorded in this passage for a reason. I believe God gave us the numbers in these 5 verses so that we can accurately continue with the dating of God's calendar. Therefore lets add up what God has given us.

Genesis 11:32 Abraham's father dies at 205 years old. Abraham was 75 (Genesis 12:4) when his dad was 205; so how old was Terah when Abraham was born? Subtract 75 from 205 and you have 130. Terah was 130 years old when Abraham born.

Since Terah was 130 years old when Abraham born, what year was Abraham born? We see in Gen 11:26 that it was 1948 when Abraham's dad was <u>70</u> and he became a father to his first son. In Genesis 11:32 through Genesis 12:4 we see that Abraham's dad died at 205 and Abraham was 75 during that time-frame. Subtracting 75 from 205 reveals that Terah was <u>130</u> years old *when Abraham was born. If we take Terah's age at Abraham's birth, which was 130, and subtract Terah's age when he had his first son, which was 70, the result is that Abraham was born 60 years after his oldest brother, 130–70=60. This information gives us the year of Abraham's birth, and a starting point to know the year of the covenant, which was 75 years later. As well as the year of the Passover, which was 430 years after the covenant of promise. So let's add all these numbers up to see the years of these events and what we can learn from this information.*

Terah's 1st born was in 1948 and adding 60 years reveals Abraham was born in the year 2008. Therefore when Abraham was 75, it was the year 2083. It was the year 2083 that Abraham turned 75 and entered the promise land. I know this is a lot of numbers to keep track of but if you can follow the numbers you will see additional proof of God's prophetic timing. Also revealed is the historic timing of what happened during that 430 years between Abraham and Moses.

God's biblical calendar reveals that Abraham entered the Promise Land in year 2083. I have shared earlier biblical evidence that later that year while Abraham was still 75 that he received the Covenant of Promise. If you add 430 years (Gal 3:17-18) to 2083 you will arrive at the year 2513. According to the numbers given in the Bible the Passover would be in year 2513. For constancy I will use the numbers from the Bible to help us get a prospective on the dating of these historic events. In reality you could have 2 different years in the same week. Therefore the exact year is not important or worth arguing about, but the 430 years between Abraham and Moses is very important and needs to be well established. According to the numbers given in Bible it was 2513 years after the creation of Adam that Israel left Egypt. Since God instructed Moses to make the month of Passover the 1st month of the year (Exodus 12:2) then it would still be 2513 when Moses received the 10 commandments at Mount Sinai.

If you properly write in and add up the dates next to the verses of God's genealogical calendar, then when you come to Genesis 47:6-9 you will see that it was year 2298. 2298 is the year Israel went into Egypt. There are 215 years between 2298 (Israel going to Egypt) and 2513 (Israel leaving Egypt), 2513-2298=215. If you take the year of 2298 (Israel arriving in Egypt) and go back and subtract 2083 (the year of the promise given to Abraham) it reveals that it was also 215 years after promise that Israel went to Egypt, 2298–2083=215.

215 is ½ of the 430 years between Abraham's promise and the Law of Moses (Gal 3:17-18). God's calendar reveals that Israel was in Egypt a total of 215 years.

If you continue to properly add and note the numbers of God's biblical calendar you will see that Joseph died 71 years after Israel went to Egypt, in the year 2369 (Gen 50:26), 2369-2298=71. This leaves 144 years that Israel remained in Egypt after Joseph, 215-71=144. Israel did not become slaves until Joseph was long gone (Exodus 1:6-11, Isaiah 52:4)

If you remove the 71 years of blessing under Joseph at the beginning of the 215 years in Egypt, then remove the 80 years of slavery during Moses' life at the end of the 215 years in Egypt; you see it leaves 64 years in the middle of the 215 years of Israel's time in Egypt.

Then remember there were years of blessing following Joseph's death and years of Israel's slave labor building the Egypt's cities Pithom and Rameses before Moses' birth. Therefore the Bible reveals that Israel was slaves in Egypt about ½ of the 215 years that they spent in Egypt.

So how are all these facts important to us? Is this significant or just useless information? Here is the Bottom line to remember.

The Bible clearly reveals that there was exactly 430 years between the 2-day convent with Abraham in Gen 15:17-18 and the Passover and departure from Egypt in Exodus 12:40-41. This 430-year time line is clearly illustrated at the end of chapter 6 in Deep Foundations. This 430-year timeline is a crucial foundation to support a clear understanding of the length of a prophetic generation (Gen 15:16, Luke 21:32). Also, it resolves the age-old debate between Calvinism and Arminianism because it illustrates how God's sovereignty and man's freewill work together. When we get to chapter 6 we will look at God's calendar of prophetic seasons and see what season we are in. Should we be preparing for the Great Tribulation or the Great Awakening? The biblical answer may surprise you.

20) Did Jesus say He would be in the grave three days and three nights?

Yes in Matthew 12:40. The Greek is just as clear as the English in stating that Jesus said He would be in the grave 3 complete 24-hour days. The Greek word Jesus used for day is "Hemera" which has 2 main definitions: 1}- a 24-hour day, 2}- daytime as opposed to nighttime. Even if you consider Friday "day time" as day 1, Saturday as day 2, there is no third daytime because the tomb was empty before is was daytime Sunday (John 20:1). Jesus said 3 days and 3 nights. The Greek word Jesus used for night is "Nyx" which simply means night or time of darkness. The Greek word Jesus used for three is "Treis" which is a plural word that is only translated as 3. It is without question that Jesus said He would be in the tomb 3 whole days. The only question is; do you believe what Jesus said or do you dispute what Jesus said (Matthew 16:21-22, Mark 8:31-32). There are some that say you can't take the Bible literally because some verses say Jesus will come out of the tomb "on the third day" and others say "after three days." Chapter 9 of the book Deep Foundations clearly explains that Jesus did rise from the dead after 3 days and it was also on the third day. The key to this riddle is that the Jewish day ended at sundown and the Gentile (Roman) day ended at midnight. Jesus knew exactly what He was saying and God's written word is accurate no contradictions.

21) How many days and nights are there between late Friday night and early Sunday morning?

There is one full day and night between late Good Friday evening and early Easter Sunday morning – a little over 24 hours. There is a Greek word for a 24-hour day; it is "nuchthemeron." This singular word is translated into 5 words in 2-Corinthians 11:25 which are "a night and a day." This was one complete day according to the Greek. Paul did not have a stopwatch but instead use the sun to tell time. Jesus did not use this word found in 2-Corinthians 11:25 because it stands for a single day, but instead Jesus made is clear that He would be in the tomb 3 complete days, which is best described as 3 days and 3 nights (Matthew 12:40).

22) **During the Passover week in the year of Jesus's crucifixion what was Wednesday called?**

*Preparation Day (John 19:14-15, Mark 15:42-43, Luke 23:53-54): The Lord's Supper happened after dark, which was the beginning of the Jewish Preparation Day. At that time Jesus introduced the New Covenant with a new Passover (Hebrews 8:6-7), feathering Himself as the Spotless Lamb, symbolized by the unleavened bread. Toward the end of Preparation Day came the time to kill all the Passover lambs. At the very same time the priest were killing the Passover lambs, Jesus died on the cross. The Passover lamb is a vivid picture of what Jesus did for us (John 1:29, Romans 6:23). In the precise timing of Jesus' death and things leading up to it, we see the fingerprints of God and proof of God's involvement. Our traditions often wipe out these details, leading many people to doubt God's Word. According to the 2017 Gallup poll, for the first time in history, more Americans believe the Bible is just a book of fairy-tales recorded by men (26%), than those that believe the Bible is the Word of God. Here is a quotation from that 2017 Gallup poll; "**Fewer than one in four Americans (24%) now believe the Bible is the actual word of God, and is to be taken literally, word for word." This is down from the (31%) reflected in the 2007 Gallup poll.** If we continue to lose 7% every 10 years, then before today's teenagers retire no one will believe the Bible is true. This will not happen because God is raising up Christian leaders that will proclaim the true Word of God, which will ignite the next Great Awakening (John 17:18-20).*

23) **During the Passover week in the year of Jesus's crucifixion what was Thursday called?**

The High Sabbath of Passover, which came after Preparation Day (Exodus 12:2-14). Preparation Day was preparation for the Passover (John 19:14). The original Passover Lamb was eaten before midnight, which is when the death angel passed over Egypt (Exodus 12:23-29).

24) **During the Passover week in the year of Jesus's crucifixion what was Friday called?**

The Holly Feast of Unleavened Bread, this feast is held on the day after the Passover (Leviticus 23:4-6). The Holly Feast of Unleavened Bread celebrated Israel's exiting Egypt (Exodus 12:17). The Pharisees would not call for judgments or crucifixions on the day they were to focus on their deliverance from slavery or the day they were to focus on their exiting Egypt (John 19:31). These days were set aside to focus on and reflect on what God has done for them.

25} **During the Passover week in the year of Jesus's crucifixion what was Saturday called?**

Saturday was the Jewish Weekly Sabbath (Exodus 16:22-26, Exodus 20:9-11) but there were also other Sabbath days in addition to Saturdays (Leviticus 23:24-25, Leviticus 23:39, John 19:31). Jesus rose from the grave after the conclusion of the Jewish weekly Sabbath. This would also be the conclusion of the third night and the third day. Jesus' words were precisely fulfilled and all 4 gospels as well as Acts and 1st Corinthians declare it with accuracy.

Further discussion questions

26} **How would you summarize this chapter?**

27} **What do you think was the most important biblical explanation to remember?**

28} **What Bible verses were the most revealing or noteworthy to you?**

29} **Can you think of ways to apply this information to your daily life?**

CHAPTER 2
ORIGINS & DEFINITIONS

30} **What is the simple definition of the word spirit?**

"Unseen motivator," this definition can be used everywhere the word spirit is found. If a definition of a word cannot be use in every place the word is found it is either inadequate or wrong.

The exception is that some words have multiple definitions. In that case the context of the passage will help you realize which definition is appropriate. The definition of a word is more important than the word itself. If Satan can confuse the definitions, he can hide what the Word is saying, resulting in blindness and deception (2-Corinthians 4:2-4). Understand and consistently applying the proper definitions to the words of the Bible unveils the true biblical portrait of God and reveals answers to life's mysteries.

31} **What is the simple definition of a soul?**

The individual person; the soul is the person you are (Acts 2:41-42$_{KJV}$). 3000 souls are 3000 individuals or 3000 people.
Some have defined the soul as only the mind, will and emotions. This definition does not distinguish the soul from the nature or an angel or God Himself, since they all have minds, wills and emotions. Also the mind, will and emotions are nothing more than thoughts but the soul is an eternal spirit. The soul can be separated from the body and still represent the individual person. (1-Thessalonians 4:13-16, Isaiah 61:10, Revelation 6:9-11). You can't put a robe on a mind, will and emotions. Another thing to understand about the soul is that the soul is feminine because it has the ability to bear the fruit of the Spirit or the fruit of the Old Man (Romans 7:4, Romans 8:11, Galatians 5:16-23, James 4:4).

32} **What is the definition used in the book Deep Foundations for the human nature?**

Nature is the species you are. God has a Divine Nature; mankind is born with a human nature. The human nature is masculine (we are not talking about males and females). The Bible often uses the physical to represent the spiritual. What I am saying is that in the Bible the man carries the authority and identity. This is what distinguishes the masculine human nature as the identity of the species and the authority given to it. The nature will give the identity to the kind of fruit the soul will bear (Matthew 7:16-20). In the Bible the human nature is called the flesh, old man, and even things like a tree that bears bad fruit or a fountain with bitter water. All these names identify some characteristic of the fallen human nature.

33) **The masculine human nature is the** _identity_ **of the species with the** _authority_ **given to it.**

34) **The "soul" is the** _person you are_, **and the "nature" is the** _species you are_.

35) **What is a simple definition of the word Grace?**

Grace is God given power. Grace is empowering favor that brings joy. It has nothing to do with whether it is earned or not. Grace is the application of God given power and ability to act and think properly with perfect timing (John 1:14, Luke 2:40). The common definitions for grace such as unmerited favor cannot be applied to these verses about Jesus because they are definitions of mercy not grace. Biblical grace is not a reference to mercy, but instead it is Godly empowerment (2-Corinthians 12:9). Grace is the root-word of graceful which has more to do with proper movement than being set free of consequences. We should pray to be full of grace (graceful) in all we do (2-Peter 3:17-18, 1-Corinthians 1:3-8).

36) **Does God micromanage everything that happens in our world?**

No, we make choices and will be healed accountable for our decisions. We cannot blame God for our bad choices. Our decisions have consequences. Many of our decisions have a compounding affect on others (Exodus 34:6-7, 2-Timothy 1:5). We cannot blame God for the bad choices other people make. We are not puppets. We were created with the power of "Free Will"(Deuteronomy 30:19, Joshua 24:15, Matthew 23:37). God established many laws at creation. We may refer to them as the laws of nature or natural law (Gen 1:11-12), "yielding seed after own kind" and reproducing after its own kind (Gen 1:21-22). These things were designed to function without God micromanaging their every move. God sustains the environment for His creation to continue, but creation was designed with the ability to function independently of God within its given parameters. As an example, lets look at one of the many natural laws: The law of gravity. Ultimately God is responsible for everything gravity does, because God created gravity. We are also responsible for how we deal with gravity. Does God make you fall when you jump off a cliff? No, gravity makes you fall. If you understand gravity, would you go base-jumping without a parachute? That is what Satan wanted Jesus to do "cast thyself down" (Matthew 4:5-7). Is it God's fault if we don't listen to His Word or heed His warnings? What we sow we will reap (Galatians 6:7). Ignorance and deception are dangerous, because there is a war between good and evil, light and darkness & there are casualties. God=good / Satan=evil (John 10:10). God does not micromanage Satan, but God does manage and restrict Satan to operate in a Sovereignty designed environment (Job 1:8-19). After Job's season with Satan he was delivered from self-righteousness and fear (Job 3:25) and then blessings and knowledge were multiplied (Job 42:12-16).

God's Word brings light (John 1:1-14, John 8:12, John 9:5). Now we are the light of the world (Matthew 5:14-16, Acts 26:18). All darkness needs to do to prevail is to hide the light of God's Word. All of us will have storms in life (John 16:33). The question is how do we act in the storm (Mark 4:37-41). Do we focus on the Storm and apply situational ethics or do we focus on what God has said and can do? God said we are going to the other side (Mark 4:35). To have peace in the storm we need get prospective (Romans 8:18). God will comfort us so we can comfort others (2-Corinthians 1:3-4).

37) **The physical world is not a** _manifestation_ **of God, It is a** _creation_ **of God.**

38) **God sustains the** _environment_ **for His creation to continue, but creation was designed with the ability to function** _independently_ _of God_ **within its given parameters.**

39) **Which part of the trinity of God is omnipresent?**

The Devil would like us to be ignorant and superstitious about God. The Bible reveals many things about God that God wants us to know and understand. To start with, the Bible reveals God has 3 parts which work together to make 1 God. The Bible also reveals that these 3 parts are distinct and different from one another. Because God is a trinity He is complete and lacking nothing. Now let's look at how the Bible distinguishes one part of the trinity of God from another. The definition of the word omnipresent is to always be present all the time. Therefore, according to the Bible, only the Father is addressed as being omnipresent in the purest sense (Psalms 139:7-12$_{KJV}$). Both Jesus and the Holy Spirit have the ability to come and go (John 16:7). Therefore, by definition, if you come and go, you cannot be omnipresent. To be consistent (as we should be in all things) we can only apply the attribute of omnipresence to the Father. However, the Father is always in contact with Jesus, therefore Jesus can be virtually with us, but in reality He is in Heaven at this time (John 14:2-3). Also there is a place where the Father is magnified which is the throne of God. Therefore when Jesus said He is going to the Father, He is going to where the Father is concentrated and making dissensions for the body (John 16:16,28, Hebrews 8:1, Hebrews 12:2, Revelation 3:21).

40) What is the advantage of being omnipresent?

Being omnipresent means you are everywhere at once. Therefore you can see everything at once, even our unseen thoughts and motivations (Ezekiel 11:5). God not only knows our thoughts but He also knows where our thoughts and motivations came from. The Father is not only omnipresent, but He is also omniscient, which means the Father already knows everything (John 14:28, Matthew 24:35-36). If you are omnipresent and omniscient then you can see the big picture, the past, present and future at the same time (Romans 4:17). If you are omnipresent, you have first hand knowledge of everything that is going on everywhere and nothing is hid from you (Jeremiah 23:24). If you are omnipresent then you constantly see all the evil just as clearly as all the good. In Ezekiel chapters 8 and 9 the omnipresent Father reveals abominations and hidden things to Jesus and Jesus comes to Ezekiel to reveal these evil things to his prophet (Ezekiel 8:6-13, Ezekiel 9:9, Proverbs 15:3, Hebrew 9:27). At Judgment day the omnipresent and omniscient God can and will reveal everything to everyone and there will be no deceptions or misunderstandings (Luke 8:17, Luke 12:2).

41) What is the advantage of not being omnipresent?

You can experience fresh new emotions as new events confront you. You can also enjoy learning new things on a firsthand experiential basis (Genesis 18:20-21). You can remove yourself from an undesirable environment (Deuteronomy 23:14). Remember that if you are omnipresent then you cannot turn away from evil or things that cause you pain. When Jesus cried out from the cross "My God why have you forsaken me" (Mark 15:34), He was not talking to the Father, because the Father can not turn away or leave the aria. Jesus was talking to the Holy Spirit which left Jesus on the cross and latter returned to raise Jesus from the dead (Romans 8:11). Also in the next few words Jesus spoke to the Father and said "Into thy hands I give my spirit (spotless human nature)," (Luke 23:46). If you were omnipresent, you would embody everything at once. I remember where I was when God first showed me this special part of His trinity. It was one morning at work, and I was standing outside my body-shop paint-booth looking in at a car. I said to God "I see the Holy Spirit is your Divine Nature and Jesus represents Your personality/Soul, but what represents the Father?" He clearly said in my heart "the Body." I responded, "how?" The answers are in the 2nd chapter of Deep Foundations.

42} What is the main attribute of the Divine Nature of God?

Holiness: Love is the main fruit, but holiness is the defining word for the Holy Spirit of God. If you look up the definition of the word "defining" it states: to define is to show the nature of something. God's Nature is first of all Holy (Isaiah 6:3, Revelation 4:8). The best definition of holiness is to purify ones self from things that defile ones personal character and conduct (2-Corinthians 7:1, 2-Timothy 2:21NIV). It involves being set apart and separated from corruption (Leviticus 20:26, 1-Peter 2:9). Corruption and rebellion grieves the Holy Spirit to the point He either turns away from it (Exodus 33:3-5) or burns the sin away (Hebrews 12:29). The Holy Spirit can turn away from corruption or burn away corruption but He will not participate in corruption. The Holy Spirit understands we are sinners and fall short of perfection. Therefore He looks at our efforts and focuses on our deliverance and empowerment (Acts 1:8). You can see the Holy Spirit as well as the other members of the trinity mentioned in 2-Peter 1:2-4. I submit that in this passage, God is a reference to the Father, Jesus is named, and the Divine Nature is a reference the Holy Spirit. 2-Peter 1:2-3 refers to the importance of the knowledge of God.

The knowledge of God's Word helps us to connect to the Divine Nature of God (2-Peter 1:4). Verses 3 and 4 reveals that we connect to the Divine Nature by receiving God's Word and then the Divine Nature empowers us to be delivered from the corruption of the world. God has a Divine Nature (Holy Spirit) and His Divine Nature comes to dwell in every believer (John 14:26). The Holy Spirit comes from the Father in name of Jesus into our heart if we ask for Him (Luke 11:13). We are born with a human nature, which the Bible calls "the flesh", but we can be born-again by receiving the Divine Nature, which give us a new identity as a child of God (Romans 8:9, 2-Corinthians 5:17). After the Holy Spirit enters our heart, He will never break His union with us because of the New Testament Covenant that Jesus established (Hebrews 12:24, Hebrews 8:6, 2-Corinthians 1:21-22, Ephesians 1:13-14, John 14:16, Romans 8:15). The Holy Spirit will be with a Christian forever, however our fellowship with Him can be diminished or enhanced (Ephesians 4:17-30). Understanding the Holy Spirit and His roll in our life makes Satan very uncomfortable. Don't let Satan blind you (as mentioned in Ephesians 4:18 and 27) to the truth about God, which is well established in the Bible.

43) Does God have a Soul, if so can you identify what part of God would be considered God's Soul?

Yes God has a Soul (Leviticus 26:11-12₍kjv₎, Isaiah 42:1₍kjv₎). Jesus literally fulfills both of these verses after he joined our human race. Jesus the King of kings left the throne room in Heaven's capital city and came to this Earth. When Jesus talks about coming and going to the Father, He is referring to Heaven's throne room where the Father is concentrated and making decisions for the Kingdom (John 16:28). Yet at the very same time Jesus was saying He was going to the Father, He then acknowledged the Father is with Him (John 16:32). Jesus joined our human race by receiving a pure human nature, which gave him a new identity as human (Hebrews 2:16-17₍KJV₎). It is the Human nature that identifies us as mankind (Acts 14:11, 15 ₍NKJV, MEV₎). Jesus is called the last Adam because only Adam and Jesus began this life with a pure human nature. Jesus the Messiah is God's only begotten son (John 3:16,18). He became God's only begotten son the day the virgin Marry conceived a son from the

Holy Spirit of God (Acts 13:33). At that time Jesus took on a new identity as a human. Jesus became human, yet He remained the eternal person of God (John 8:58, John 17:5, John 17:24). We called Him Emmanuel "God with us" (Matthew 1:23). Jesus the Messiah is 100% Soul of God and 100% nature of man.

JESUS

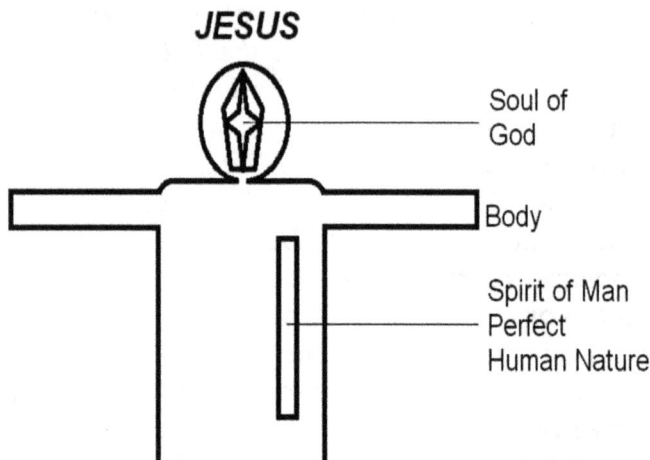

Soul of God

Body

Spirit of Man
Perfect
Human Nature

Only Jesus qualifies to fit the description of the Soul (person) of God (John 14:7-9, John 1:18, 1-John 4:12). Jesus reveals the personality of the Father. This is covered in detail in chapter 5 of the book Deep Foundations.

44) Does it matter if God has a soul?

Yes, because having a soul reveals God is a person not an inanimate force. Having a soul reveals God has feelings. Consistently applying all the definitions found in this book helps us to see what each word is saying. God is a person with His own Soul (Personality) and His own Nature (Divine Nature). There is one God and He is revealed in the Bible as a trinity. We are created in His likeness as a trinity (Genesis 1:26-27). Understanding the trinity will reveal how and why biblical salvation works. The trinity of man and what has happened to it, will be illustrated in Chapters 3 and 4 of the book Deep Foundations. These insights are used through the book to help us realize the transformation that is necessary for us to qualify to be a part of God's perfect paradise of Heaven.

45) What is a definition of the word meekness?

Meekness is to have our power under the control of the proper authority. Jesus was meek because His power was under the Father's authority (John 12:49-50, Luke 22:42). Jesus was meek because His enormous power was also submitted to the authority of the scriptures (Matthew 26:53-54). Jesus is our best example of meekness (Matthew 11:29$_{KJV}$). It is good to be meek (Matthew 5:5$_{KJV}$).

46} **What is an illustration of the word meekness?**

It's like a powerful wild high-spirited horse that has been trained to trust the rider to choose the direction and speed to go by a simple gesture of the reins.

Further discussion questions

47} **How would you summarize this chapter?**

48} **What do you think was the most important biblical explanation to remember?**

49} **What Bible verses were the most revealing or noteworthy to you?**

50} **Can you think of ways to apply this information to your daily life?**

CHAPTER 3
THE FALL

51} **What does it mean to say God is Sovereign?**

The phrase God is Sovereign means nobody rules over God. God determines our boundaries (Acts 17:26-28). God establishes the rules within those boundaries. God is ultimately in control of everything. However as discussed in question 36, God does not micromanage our every move or circumstance.

52} **What are Satan's three powerful weapons of mass destruction?**

The lust of the flesh, the lust of the eyes, the pride of life are Satan's three powerful weapons of mass destruction (1-John 2:16). The Devil used these weapons on Eve. Genesis 3:6, good for food = lust of the flesh, pleasant to the eye = lust of the eyes, make one wise = pride of life. Devil used these same weapons on Jesus. Luke 4:3 eat = lust of the flesh, Luke 4:5-7 shewed unto Him = lust of the eyes, Luke 4:9-11 = too important to be disabled = pride of life. The Devil will use these weapons on you and me. He may focus on one weapon or change up the order as he did with Jesus in Matthew 4:1-11.

53} What are Satan's weapons fueled with?

Deception (Revelation 12:9, 2-Corinthians 11:13-15)

54} What is the definition and origin of the word sin?

The definition of sin comes from an old archery term. The amount of "sin" was the distance by which your arrow missed the center of the target. To sin means you missed it, or have fallen short (Romans 3:23). If you miss the point, it is sin (Romans 14:23). We sin a lot more than we realize (1-John 1:5-10).

55} What is the definition of the word transgression?

Transgression is to break the law (Romans 4:15).

56} Who transgressed first Adam or Eve?

Eve (Genesis 3:6)

57} Did Eve sin before she ate the fruit of the forbidden tree?

Yes - she misquoted God's word saying God said she could not even touch the forbidden fruit. God's instruction to Adam was not to consume the forbidden fruit (Genesis 3:3, Genesis 2:17). Sometimes small sins lead to big transgressions.

58} What died when Adam and Eve transgressed by eating the forbidden fruit?

The human nature died that day (Ephesians 2:1-3)

59} What happened to their heart after they eat the fruit of the forbidden tree?

The light went out and their heart became dark (Romans 1:21)

60} **Adam and Eve tried to cover up their nakedness because of shame, but how else did sin affect their perceptions?**

They began to fear (Genesis 3:9-10). They tried to hide from God and no longer wanted to walk and talk with God (Genesis 3:8). They also began to blame others for their bad choices (Genesis 3:12-13)

61} **The antidote for shame is found in understanding Romans 8:1 and 2-Corinthians 5:17; but where is the antidote for fear found?**

1-John 4:18 - Love is the antidote for fear

62} **Who did the fallen human race come from, Adam or Eve?**

In the Bible, we trace our personal sin nature back to Adam, not to Eve even though she sinned first (Romans 5:12, Romans 5:19, 1-Corinthians 15:21-22).

63} **Can the fallen human nature be redeemed?**

No, the human nature died that day in the Garden of Eden, and its destiny was sealed for eternity. The human nature " is not subject to the law of God, <u>neither indeed can be</u>" (Romans 8:7). The human nature, which is often called "the flesh <u>cannot please God</u>" (Romans 8:8). The Calvinistic doctrine of total depravity only applies to the fallen human nature. Only the fallen human nature is dead and unable to respond to God. Where Calvinism goes wrong is that God does not wake up (regenerate) the dead human nature but instead replaces it with a new nature, which the Bible refers to as the Divine Nature (2-Peter 1:4). This union of the Divine Nature and our Soul is referred to as the New Man (Ephesians 4:17-24, Colossians 3:9-10). Every soul has an ability and opportunity to receive the Divine Nature in their heart (John 1:9), which will make them a new creation (2-Corinthians 5:17). This is referred to as being born again (John 3:3, John 3:7, 1-Peter 1:23). If we are being born then we are "children of God" (Romans 8:16, Romans 8:21 Romans 9:8, Galatians 3:26).

64} **Can a defiled woman birth an undefiled child?**

Yes, if the father is undefiled, because we inherit our fallen human nature from our fathers (1-Corinthians 15:21-22, Romans 5:12, Romans 5:19).

65} What came first the chicken or the egg?

The chicken and it was able to bear fruit of its own kind (species). Meaning you may find a variety of chicken eggs but there are no chickens laying snake eggs (Genesis 1:21-27). Also God created many things mature (with age built in). For instance the starlight did not take years to reach the Earth (Genesis 1:16-17).

66} In Genesis when did God begin and end the daily cycle?

The beginning of the night (darkness) started the daily cycle (Genesis 1:5)

67} What day did God create the 24-hour lunar-day?

The 4th day God created the lunar-day, which ended at sunset (Genesis 1:14-19).

68} Is there an exception to the 24-hour lunar-day?

In northern Alaska, the daytime could last for months before the night concludes it. "Residents of Barrow enjoy the midnight sun all summer - over 80 days of uninterrupted daylight." The Earth has gone though many changes after it was created. In the beginning the Earth was like a greenhouse with a water canopy where our Ozone layer is now (Genesis 1:7-8, Genesis 7:11-12). Therefore, there was no polar icecaps until after Noah's flood, which began the ice-age in some places. It is unlikely that the 6th day of creation was a 24 hour day. We can see this by reading Genesis 1:24-31 and the elaboration of the events on the 6th day in Genesis 2:7-8 and Genesis 2:15-23. It would be hard to realistically cram all these events into a 12 hour day or even if you include the night, a 24 hour day. God's first 6 days began and ended in the evening. These days ended at the beginning of the darkness, not at the end of 24 hours. Therefore the 6th day could last for months and easily have plenty of time to include all the events that happened that day as listed in Geneses. Don't forget God can and has made adjustments to our 24 hour day in the past (Joshua 10:12-13, 2-Kings 20:10-11). Whether its by miracle or by design God is not limited to a 24 hour day. When you have your eyes open to the facts, you can see that the Bible is true and makes sense. You can see it is impossible to have a creation without a creator. The complexity and precision of our Ecosystem and life itself could never happen by a series accidents.

Further discussion questions

69} **How would you summarize this chapter?**

70} **What do you think was the most important biblical explanation to remember?**

71} **What Bible verses were the most revealing or noteworthy to you?**

72} **Can you think of ways to apply this information to your daily life?**

CHAPTER 4
THE HEART OF THE MATTER

73} **The heart is a** _transmitter_ **of** _information_**.**

According to the Bible, the heart is not just the seat of emotions, but it is also the conveyor of information. When the Bible says their "Heart was not right" as in Psalm 78:37 or Acts 8:21, God is commenting on their thinking not their emotions.

74} **Who is in charge of what remains in our heart?**

Our soul. In other words, we are (Luke 6:45, Matthew 6:21, Proverbs 4:23). We are to guard our heart. We need to avoid meditating on ungodly thoughts. Everyone has ungodly thoughts, but we need to uproot them before they grows into ungodly attitudes and actions. Satin and our old nature is constantly trying to sow weed-seeds in our heart. We need to uproot them and plant good seed in our heart (2-Corinthians 10:5). We do this by meditating on the Word of God (Ephesians 5:26, Romans 12:2).

75} Can our heart be divided and communicate mixed messages?

Yes (Psalm 12:2₍ₖⱼ₎, James 4:8, Matthew 22:37-40) The Devil wants to establish strongholds in or heart from which he can bring darkness to our heart and pollute our soul (Romans 1:21-32).

76} How is the heart different from the soul?

Heart is the driveway to get to the soul. The heart contains information. The soul is your personality. The heart is like a computer connected to the Internet and the soul is like the person operating the computer and searching out information. Even though the computer may present some unwanted popup adds or corrupting web-pages on its screen, it is the person at the keyboard that has the ability to change what is on the computer screen. It is up to the person at the keyboard to choose whether he focuses on the good or the evil and operates with a split screen or a full screen. The soul chooses what remains in the heart, but what remains in the heart will affect the soul either positively or negatively (Isaiah 32:6, Proverbs 2:10).

77} How is the heart different from the human nature?

The human nature is the identity of the species and the authority giving to it. The heart is a transmitter of information. The heart can be transformed. The human nature cannot be regenerated or redeemed. The heart and soul are redeemable but the fallen human nature will never change. The fallen human nature has many names, but its identity is the Old Man. Its fate is forever sealed in death and corruption. The doctrine of total depravity and the inability to respond to God applies to the fallen human nature, which is referred to in the Bible as the "Old Man," (Ephesian 4:17-22) or the "Flesh" (Romans 8:5-8). Some modern translations use the words "sinful nature" instead of flesh. The flesh (fallen human nature) not only will not, but "CAN NOT" please or respond to God. The fallen human nature is "not subject to the law of God, NEITHER INDEED CAN BE." Those controlled by the this fallen nature will reject God and have their heart darken with deception (Romans 1:21-22). On the other hand, God can come into our dark heart and transform it by giving us light (2-Corinthians 4:6, John 1:9). Every person without exception receives God's light of truth in their heart (Romans 1:19-20). After the light of truth and salvation enters the heart, our soul will have an opportunity to make a choice (Deuteronomy 30:19). Everyone will be held accountable for their decision (Galatians 6:7, Hebrews 9:27, Jeremiah 17:10). The bottom line is every Soul can be saved. Every heart can be transformed. Every sinful nature will end up in the Lake of Fire. Everyone has an opportunity to receive transformation by receiving the Divine Nature of Jesus in their heart. The Divine Nature will replace the human nature making us fit for Heaven.

78) **Draw a diagram that reveals a Christian's natures, heart and soul.**

Christian

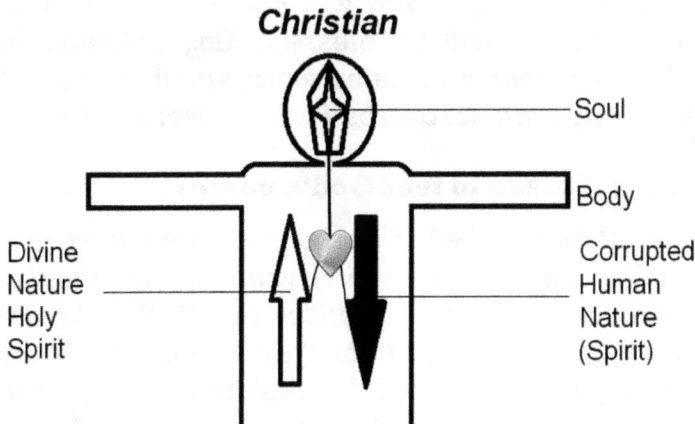

79) **Do we need to be naive to have a pure heart?**

No, God wants us to be wise, analytical and discerning (Matthew 10:16, Proverbs 13:1, Proverbs 1:5, Proverbs 2:10-14). A wise person is not naive or fooled by deceptive traps (1-John 4:1). A wise person seeks out the truth and tests the information to verify its value and proper application (3-John 1:4). A pure heart is not prejudice against the true but instead will follow the facts to their conclusions. A pure heart doesn't have an ungodly bias, but looks for the proper balance and purpose of the information.

80) **What is Satan's main objective in dealing with our heart?**

To keep God's Word from taking root in our heart (Matthew 13:19, Ephesians 4:18, Luke 8:12-14). The Devil is doing what we *need to do, except he is uprooting the seeds of God and we need to uproot the seeds from Satan.*

81) **What is the first step in being set free of blinding deceptions?**

We need to open our heart up to the Light of Biblical Truth in order to receive correction and instruction (John 8:32). You start with knowing the truth. It is not enough to just know the truth, you need to know how to properly apply the truth and that takes wisdom (Proverbs 2:6, James 1:5-8). God ask Solomon what was the one thing He wanted (1-Kings 3:4-5). Solomon ask for wisdom (1-Kings 3:9-12, 1-Kings 10:24,23). Who was Solomon's mother? Bathsheba, so it doesn't mater what your past mistakes are, or your family history is, if you will spend time with God and apply His word you will be blessed. *King Solomon wrote the book of Proverbs which contains more about wisdom than any other book of the Bible (Proverbs 16:16, Proverbs 19:8).*

82) **What does it mean to fear God's name?**

We should not be terrified of God or His name. If we continually disrespect God's name and use it in vain, then we should fear the consequences (Exodus 20:7, Leviticus 22:32). We should not say things like "OMG," "my god" or "Jesus" without thought or as slang words (Deuteronomy 5:11, Matthew 12:36). Instead we should reverently respect God's name and title and use them as references to our creator (Nehemiah 9:5-6, Psalm 103:1, Psalm 105:3). We should lovingly and joyfully consider references to God to be set apart as Holy, special and precious, but not to the extent that we avoid using God's name. With respect and purpose we should use God's name regularly (Matthew 6:9). God's name is a shelter for salvation (Proverbs 18:10, Psalm 124:8) God's name and title represent God and His kingdom and His authority (Ephesians 6:11-13). God's name gives His children their identity (Acts 11:26). The first part of the word Christian is Christ. Christians are Christ-ones. Everything we do should be done as representing God's family (James 2:7) and God's good name and reputation (Colossians 3:17).

83) **What is the result of rejecting God's Word?**

All who reject God's Word remain in darkness (Ezekiel 12:2, Jeremiah 5:21, Proverbs 8:36). Closing our eyes to any part of God's Word allows Satan to start deceiving us in that aria. The seed of deception will affect other arias of our heart like a virus. The Bible refers to this influential proliferation as leaven (Mark 8:15-18, Galatians 5:9, 1-Corinthians 5:6). Satan will attempt to build strongholds in out heart in-order to take control of our heart (Jeremiah 17:9). That is why we need to monitor what is coming out of our heart (Luke 11:35, 2-Corinthians 10:5). Not understanding God's Word is not the same as rejecting God's Word. Nobody understands everything in God's Word except God. The things we do not understand we should keep in the back of our mind and wait for God to give us revelation in that aria. God has much He wants to teach us, but learning is a process that takes time (John 16:12, 1-Peter 2:2, 1-Corinthians 3:2, John 14:26). Sometimes being faithful even though we don't understand something is a test of our faith and trust in God. We see this in John 6:54-57. This was a shocking statement that is hard to understand or forget. Therefore most of Jesus' disciples rejected Him (John 6:66-67). We know Jesus did not endorse cannibalism, so why did Jesus say this? The Bible gives us the context and background to this statement. This was near the time of the Passover which symbolized Jesus the spotless lamb dying for us (John 6:4, John 1:29). Jesus miraculously fed 5,000 men as well as their wives and children. Afterward the disciples gathered up 12 baskets of leftover bread. The fish were gone because they would spoil and corrupt the bread (John 6:10-15). The crowd wanted to force Jesus into overthrowing Rome and being their king. Jesus left the aria (John 6:24-31). The crowd found Jesus, ask for another sign and brought up the manna miracle. Then we come to the hard statement by Jesus, which broke up the crowd. Jesus gave us the key to understand what He was saying (John 6:63, John 6:33-35). Jesus was emphasizing the importance and benefit to receiving His Holy Spirit. The keys to understanding confusing things in God's Word are found in God's Word (Isaiah 28:9-10, 2-Peter 1:20). I did not understand 1-Thessalonians 5:23 for years. It challenged my understanding about our human spirit (nature) being unredeemable and unable to please God. Then in 2014 God gave me revelation on that verse. God showed me that Deuteronomy 6:5 was a parallel verse. *That revelation inspired this chapter about the Heart in the book Deep Foundations.*

84} What does the term circumcision of the heart refer to?

The term circumcision of the heart refers to the removal or denial of the fallen human nature, so it does not bear fruit in our heart. The term is found in Romans 2:29, and in Colossians 2:10-11.

85} What is ground zero in the battle between good and evil?

The heart (Proverbs 4:23, Luke 6:45, Proverbs 16:9, Luke 11:35, Matthew 22:37-40, James 2:8)

Further discussion questions

86} How would you summarize this chapter?

87} What do you think was the most important biblical explanation to remember?

88} What Bible verses were the most revealing or noteworthy to you?

89} Can you think of ways to apply this information to your daily life?

CHAPTER 5
THE LAST ADAM – THE GOD-MAN

90} Beside God having a human body, how else could Jesus be 100% God and 100% man at the same time?

The Son of God, is a combination of 100% Soul of God with 100% pure nature of man.

91} Why was Jesus referred to as the last Adam?

One reason is because Adam and Jesus are the only men to begin this life with a perfect spotless human nature. Adam corrupted his human nature. In contrast Jesus' human nature remained pure. Another reason is because from Jesus will come a new race of descendants (1-Corinthians 15:21-22), not physically born, but born-again of the Spirit (John 3:3, 1-Peter 1:23, John 1:1-4). As Christians we are impacted by both the first Adam when we are born and the last Adam when we are born-again (John 3:5). We are descendants of the first Adam. Therefore we are "living souls_KJV" and members of the human race. When we are born-again we receive from the "last Adam" a new "life giving Spirit_NKJV" which makes us members of the family of God (1-Corinthians 15:45).

92} Why did Jesus have to be virgin born?

Jesus was virgin born to avoid contamination from a fallen human father. We inherit our human nature from our father going all the way back to Adam (Romans 5:12). Jesus' human nature was not a descendant of Adam, but instead was a new creation of God (Luke 1:34-35, Matthew 1:20-25). Therefore Jesus' human nature was not sinful like our human nature (Isaiah 53:6). Jesus' human nature was pure and uncontaminated (1-Peter 1:18-19, John 1:29).

93} What did Jesus inherit from his mother?

Jesus received from His mother Mary His body (Hebrews 10:5). Genesis 3:15_KJV is a reference to Jesus being virgin born of a woman, "seed" of the woman, not the seed of man. From Mary Jesus inherited His Jewish bloodline (Luke 3:23-34). Luke has the list of Mary's blood line. Matthew has a list of Joseph's blood line with Jacob being the father of Joseph (Matthew 1:16). The difference between these two list may be a little confusing but to understand Luke's genealogy look closely at the wording in Luke 3:23. Remember in the Bible the identity is with the man or sons not the daughters. Jesus "was supposed the son of Joseph," but actually "was the son of Heli" because Heli was the last male descendant before Jesus. Heli was Mary's father and Jesus' grandfather.

94} Can a sinful mother conceive and give birth to a sinless child?

Yes, because we inherit our sinful nature from our father not our mother. The source of out sinful nature goes back to Adam not Eve even though Eve sinned first (Romans 5:12). We also see in the Bible that a non-Jewish mother can have a Jewish baby because the Identity comes from the father. For instance Rahab was a Canaanite and Ruth was a Moabite and their children were Jewish. These Gentile women are listed in the royal line of king David (Matthew 1:5-6). There was never a question about if David was a Jew or not. On the other hand Timothy had a Jewish mother and a Gentile father and was not considered to be a true Jew (Acts 16:1-3).

95} Who was Jesus' actual father?

God the Holy Spirit is Jesus' father (Luke 1:35). The Holy Spirit is not defined as Jew or Gentile. Therefore as far as Jesus' ancestry goes, He was a descendant of His grandfather Heli. Therefore Jesus was Jewish because His last male relative was Heli and he was Jewish.

96} Where did Jesus' family go when they left Bethlehem?

Jerusalem (Luke 2:21-22). The Lord guided Moses in writing the first five books of the Bible. The Jews of Jesus' time were well acquainted with the Law of Moses. It was a guide for Jesus' parents. On the eighth day, Jesus was circumcised in Bethlehem in accordance with the law. By looking at the Law of Moses we can see that the family remained in Bethlehem a little over a month (Leviticus 12:1-2,4). This was a total of 40 days for the mother's purification. 40 is a significant number in the Bible. 40 is the number for transition. Israel was 40 years in the wilderness as they transitioned from a rebellious slave mentality to being obedient conquerors at Jericho. Jesus was 40 days in the wilderness as He transitioned from being a son of a carpenter to being a rabbi and miracle worker. On the eighth day of the mother's 40 days of purification the male child was to be circumcised (Leviticus 12:3). After the 40 days of purification are completed the parents were to bring a sacrifice to the temple (Leviticus 12:6-8). After Jesus was 40 days old, Mary and Joseph went 5 miles north to Jerusalem to fulfill their duty according to the law (Luke 2:22). They went to the temple in Jerusalem to dedicate Jesus unto God (Luke 2:23) and offer their sacrifice (Luke 2:24). While they were at the temple in Jerusalem, Jesus was prophesied over by Simeon and Anna (Luke 2:33).

97} Where was Jesus living 3 months after His birth?

In a house in Nazareth (Luke 2:39). Joseph was a carpenter and built the house they would live in before marrying Mary. Here is a quote from the book Deep Foundations, "It was Jewish tradition that, between the proposal and the wedding, the man would build a special place for his wife. I'm sure Joseph was excited about building their home and anticipating the day when Mary would join him there. After the bridal chamber (called the "huppah") was finished, the father of the groom would set the wedding date. I believe there is an exciting spiritual picture behind this tradition. If you search "Jewish Bridegroom" or "Jewish Wedding Traditions in Bible Times," you will find many interesting details that parallel our salvation. The key elements are that Jesus came to Earth to initiate a way for us to join His family (the engagement covenant). Now He is in Heaven preparing our eternal home there (John 14:2-3). At the Father's command, Jesus will return to bring His bride (the redeemed) home for the wedding (Revelation 19:7)."

98} Where were the wise men at the time of Jesus' birth?

Far away to the east

99} Define the Greek word translated as east.

Rising of light, which is usually in the east. This same definition for east was used by Isaiah in Isaiah 45:6 and Isaiah 59:19.

100} Where was Jesus' unusual birth-star located when the wise-men first seen it?

From the wise-men's prospective it was on the western horizon in the direction of Jerusalem. If you were a shepherd near Bethlehem it would be above your head (Luke 2:8-15). Bethlehem is five miles south of Jerusalem. The shepherds were tending the sheep in the fields between Jerusalem and Bethlehem. It is believed that these were not ordinary shepherds or sheep. These were the lambs that were used in the temple sacrifices in Jerusalem.

101} Name 2 Bible verses the wise-men could use to identify this strange light they saw in the night.

Isaiah 11:1, Numbers 24:17, both of these verses refer to a rod or scepter coming up out of Israel. This was a rod of light, which was referred to as "a Star out of Jacob." It probably got their attention because of its unusual brightness and the way it looked like an expanding shooting star, except it was rising up from the western horizon. Then the light shot away into the heavens and was gone (Luke 2:13-15). The Wise-men from the east told Herod they seen light arise from the western horizon. Some Bible translations quote them saying they "saw his star when it rose" while others say "seen his star in the east" (Matthew 2:2). Understanding the Greek word translate as east clears up the confusion and verifies the light was on the horizon not above the wise-men's heads.

102} How long did it take the wise-men to arrive in Jerusalem after seeing the star?

About 2 years (Matthew 2:16): They first took time to solve the mystery of what the star meant. They ultimately discovered two arias of the Jewish Bible that described this event and revealed its significance. They discussed the proper gifts to bring to such a significant leader, and who would accompany them. Finally after all the provisions and protections were made they set out on their journey to Jerusalem.

103} Did the wise-men find Jesus in Bethlehem?

No, Jesus was not in Bethlehem. Jesus had been living in Nazareth for about 2 years (Luke 2:39-40)

104} How did the wise-men finally find where Jesus was living?

The angel (referred to as a star) redirected them to Nazareth and pointed out the exact house where Jesus was living at that time (Matthew 2:9-11). This proves that this star was an angel with the ability to be recognized by the wise-men as a pillar of light standing on the horizon. Then just as the pillar of fire lead the Israelites though the wilderness (Nehemiah 9:19), this pillar of light redirected the wise men to head north to Nazareth, which was more than a 60 mile journey. This journey ended when the angel stood on, or pointed out the specific roof of the house where Jesus was living at that time.

105} **Proverbs 8:11 states that wisdom is extremely valuable, therefore what is wisdom, and why is it valuable?**

Wisdom is knowing how to apply truth properly. Wisdom helps us to see the truth clearly. Wisdom also understands inconsistencies that fool many people into making poor decisions. The Holy Spirit will speak words of wisdom to us (Matthew 2:12). It is wise to listen to God and read God's Word. As we read God's Word, we develop ears to hear and eyes to see what God is saying to us. Wisdom helps us to recognize the value or hazards of the different paths before us. We need wisdom to make the proper decisions (Matthew 2:13-15). Our decisions have ramifications on us as well as others. Wisdom enables us to sow the proper seed at the proper time in order to see a bountiful harvest of blessings. Wisdom helps us to realize what we sow (good or bad) we will eventually reap (Galatians 6:7). God wants all His children to be wise.

106} **How do we gain or increase wisdom?**

Ask God in faith for wisdom (James 1:5-6), then seek out God's Word and ask God to reveal His will and His ways (Proverbs 3:5-6, Psalm 32:8). Then apply the wisdom God gives you and God will increase your wisdom and knowledge (James 1:22-25, Mark 4:23-25, Matthew 13:15-16, Matthew 13:11-12).

Further discussion questions

107} **How would you summarize this chapter?**

108} **What do you think was the most important biblical explanation to remember?**

109} **What Bible verses were the most revealing or noteworthy to you?**

110} **Can you think of ways to apply this information to your daily life?**

CHAPTER 6
GOD'S SOVEREIGNTY –

MAN'S FREEWILL

111) What is a good definition of the word repent?

In the Webster Dictionary, the number one definition is "to turn from sin and dedicate oneself to the amendment of one's life." This is a common interpretation of the word repent. But in reality does the word repent have anything to do with sin? No, not in the purest sense of the word (Acts 20:21 KJV). You can repent from, something like sin. Or you can repent to, something or someone like God. A good single word equivalent for the word repent is to turn. You can turn from, and at the same time you are turning to someone, something, or a different way of thinking. Webster's second definition is more universally consistent but still lacks in the full sense of the word. Webster second definition is: "to change one's mind." The end result or completion of the word repent is to take action in another direction. This begins with a decision to go another way, and then it is followed by an action based on that decision. To make a decision without a follow-through action is not true repentance, nor is doing something different without giving it a thought. True biblical repentance includes both thought and deed (Revelation 2:4-5). Can God repent? Yes. In Jonah 3:8-10 KJV the action was to grant them a pardon, that they be not destroyed. God knew that Nineveh would not change without realizing they would be judged for their actions. God also knew Jonah would run (Jonah 4:2). God did not make Jonah rebel and run. Jonah of his own free will disobeyed. Then Jonah of his own free will repented. Then God used Jonah's unique situation to better prepared him to deliver a message that the Ninevites would take seriously and not kill him (Romans 8:28). It does not matter where we are in life, even if we are in bondage and being consumed by our circumstances, if we turn to God, He can set us free and uniquely empower us to fulfill our calling.

112) Are God's blessings and condemnations conditional and therefore changeable?

Yes, they are based on our actions in response to His Word during our time (1-Corinthians 11:31, Jeremiah 18:7-10 KJV). Jeremiah was written about a 150 years after Jonah. God was clarifying that Nineveh was not an isolated situation. The same principal applies to all people and nations. The book Deep Foundations has a statement that clarifies this, here is that quote: "You can adjust your action according to the moving target. If you didn't adjust and refocus, you would miss the target; and that would be sin as defined earlier. God never sins. His eye is always on the target, and His actions are true." God's Word is clear that God can change His actions to fit the current conditions. But how can an all-knowing sovereign God change his mind? To understand this we need to understand the trinity which is explained in the earlier chapters. In the trinity of God, the Father is omnipresent and all-knowing but Jesus and the Holy Spirit can come and go. Jesus realizes the big picture of the past, present and future but He is completely in the moment (John 11:35). His feelings change and therefore His thoughts can change (Genesis 6:5-7). God does not create anyone to go to Hell (2-Peter 3:9). The Father knows the future of every person but Jesus and the Holy Spirit are actively working to save every person and Not Willing that ANY shall perish. At one point in time they will change their mind and be willing that some perish and be condemned to an eternity in the Lake of Fire (Revelation 20:15). In conclusion the Father exists in all of eternity at the same time and there is nothing the Father does not already know or has not already seen (Jeremiah 23:24). Who is speaking here? The Father. The Father sees all because He is everywhere (Proverbs 15:3). There is nothing that the Father does not already know (Matthew 24:36). Therefore the Father cannot have a new emotion or thought which would cause Him to change His mind. On the other hand the Father can experience new feelings and fresh thoughts through the other 2 parts of the trinity of God. Jesus has always existed, but Jesus lives in the present. If Jesus currently lived in the future as well, He would know the time of His return to Earth (Mark 13:32). Jesus is not currently living in the past but He remembers the past (Luke 10:18). Jesus has always lived in the moment and able to go from place to place (John 14:2-3) and learn new things (Genesis 18:20-21) and able to be emotionally moved by the moment (Luke 7:9). Therefore He can change his mind (Jeremiah 18:7-10). Jesus' every decision is sinless and righteous and made according to the circumstances (Matthew 23:37), in light of the bigger picture (Luke 22:42).

Was Jonah swallowed by a whale or a fish?

A fish, especially prepared by God (Jonah 1:17). In Matthew 12:40, Jesus did not call this a whale, Jesus called this a "kētos" which is better translated as a great or huge fish with a large gaping mouth. The reason why some translations use the word whale is because when the Tyndale Bible of 1534 and the King James Bible of 1611 were translated, it was believed that whales were fish. They believed that a whale was a huge fish with a large gaping mouth. By the way, the King James New Testament as well as the book of Jonah is acutely the Tyndale Bible with the spelling improved and a few words changed. The King James translators compared the original manuscripts to the Tyndale translation and only changed a few words. For example they changed the word congregation to church. William Tyndale was gifted and anointed by God to translate the Bible from the original languages of Hebrew and Greek to English. He was killed in England as a martyr because he would not stop translating the Bible to English. He was burned at a stake before he could finish the Old Testament. His talent and dedication makes me consider the King James Bible as an anointed translation, in spite of some misspelling and a few words that could be refined. Calling whales fish and the misspelled words where not considered wrong at the time the King James Bible was published.

114) **Did Jonah die in the belly of the sea monster?**

Yes, Jonah's soul left his body, just as Jesus' Soul left His body (Jonah 2:2$_{KJV}$, Matthew 12:40). Before Jesus' resurrection, Hell had at least 2 parts. This is explained in chapter 11 of the book Deep Foundations. Jesus talked about two parts of Hell in Luke 16:19-26. Jonah's soul went to the waiting in comfort side of Hell. Yet Jonah's soul was tormented by his rebellious actions of rejecting God's plan for his life. Jonah focused on the temple of God and prayed (Jonah 2:4). Two things to notice in this verse. First we see that the Bible accurately quotes Jonah speaking his feelings, which where not entirely accurate. Jonah was not out of the sight of God (Psalm 139:7-8$_{KJV}$, Proverbs 15:3). The Father is everywhere, all of the time. The Father is even in the Lake of Fire to maintain it and insure that it does not get out of hand or cease to exist (Revelation 20:10, 14). If the Father was not in the Lake of Fire, then the Father would not be omnipresent. That is part of being omnipresent. Jesus visited Hell in 30 AD, but neither Jesus nor the Holy Spirit will ever be in the Lake of Fire. To depart from God is to be separated from Jesus and the Holy Spirit (Matthew 25:41). The second point starts with a question. Why did Jonah focused on the temple? The temple was a symbol of God's presence on Earth, a place where prayers were answered and miracles happened (1-Kings 9:3). This promise was conditional (1-Kings 9:6-7). God answered Jonah's prayer and delivered his body to the shore (Jonah 2:10) and returned his soul to his body so he could fulfill his mission from God (Jonah 3:1-2).

115} **Why did Jesus go into the temple and violently turn over tables and drive out merchants and animals?**

The merchants were shortchanging and taking advantage of the people for profit. Therefore, instead of having a reputation of being a house of prayer and miracles, the temple became a place where people were being ripped off (Mark 11:17).

116} **How many times did Jesus cleanse the temple in this manner?**

Jesus cleansed the temple 3 times: once at the beginning of His ministry (John 2:14-15) and twice at the end of His earthly ministry (Matthew 21:12-13, Mark 11:15-17). The context reveals that Matthew and Mark refer to two different times. Matthew was before Jesus condemned the fig tree (Matthew 21:17-19). Mark was after Jesus condemned the fig tree (Mark 11:12-15).

117} **Did Jesus foresee and expound on the temple's destruction?**

Yes, in Matthew 24:1-2 Jesus revealed that the temple building was temporary and would be removed after his crucifixion. It was destroyed just as He foretold in 70 AD, 40 years after Jesus was crucified. There were two reasons for the temple's destruction. One reason is that the temple had become corrupted and fruitless, thus His statement that it had become a "den of thieves" (Matthew 21:13). The other is the ultimate reason. The temple represented the Old Covenant, but God was introducing a New Covenant (Hebrews 10:9-10). Jesus fulfilled the law (Matthew 5:17) and concluded the Old Covenant at His crucifixion

(Hebrews 9:6-15). Jesus died for our atonement as the sacrificial Lamb of God (John 1:29). Jesus as our High Priest entered the Holy of Holies to offer Himself as the final offering to pay for our sins (Hebrews 9:24). At Jesus' death, God tore open the temple's veil of separation (Matthew 27:50-51) revealing that the temple and its sacrifices had become obsolete. The priest no longer needed to go into the Holy of Holies on the Day of Atonement to make an interest payment, because Jesus payed off the sin debt (John 19:30). the Greek word translated as finish is tetelestai, which was the word written on receipts to show a bill or debt had been paid in full.

Something else was also revealed. The Ark of the Covenant was missing (Hebrews 9:5). Historians believe it was hid during the time of Jeremiah before Babylon invaded Jerusalem. Jeremiah spoke of its removal in Jeremiah 3:16.

Here is some background and history of the Ark of the Covenant which was topped with the Mercy Seat. God directed Moses in the building and placement of the Ark (Exodus 25:9-22, Exodus 26:33-34, Exodus 25:40, Hebrews 9:24). The Ark was a powerful representation of God. It was not just a religious artifact, as you can see in 1-Samuel chapters 5 and 6. There is some confusing about the number in 1-Samuel 6:19. The population of the city Beth Shemesh at that time was probably much less than 50,070. Here's a couple of interpretations to clear up the confusion. The Hebrew word eh'·lef which is translated as 1000 can also refer to oxen. Here is a quote from the Strong's Lexicon: "אֶלֶף 'eleph, eh'-lef; prop, the same as H504; hence (the ox's head being the first letter of the alphabet, and this eventually used as a numeral) a thousand." The Hebrew word 'eleph evolved as time passed. It started out as a word for Ox or bull. As time past because it was also the first letter in the Hebrew alphabet it was used for a leader or captain. To be a leader there needs to be a clan or followers, therefore the word included both the leader and the followers. That is where the number of followers came into question and became 100 then 1000. Eventually the word was used as the number 1000 or an expression of a purposeful exaggeration for effect, like we would say "I have a million things to do." Therefor the word 'eleph needs to be interpreted by the context to determine if it is an exaggeration or a specific number of a 100 or a 1000 or is referring to a bull or ox. The New King James Version refers to this in their footnote: "Or He struck seventy men of the people and fifty oxen of a man." Therefore this verse could read: "Then He struck the men of Beth Shemesh, because they had looked into the ark of the LORD. He struck fifty oxen and seventy men of the people, and the people lamented because the LORD had struck the people with a great slaughter." The other explanation is as some translators write "He struck down of all the people, 50,070 men." This would include the 5 divisions of the Philistine territory listed in the previous 2 verses. I believe the context of this verse points to this explanation. The 50,070 was the total number of people that died which were mostly Philistines (1-Samuel 5:6-12).

No one was to touch the Ark (2-Samuel 6:6-7). That is why it had rings attached to it and poles for the priest to carry it (1-Chronicles 15:11-15). The Ark would latter be placed in the most holy place of Solomon's temple (1-Kings 8:1-11). The Ark remained there until time of Jeremiah. It is believed that before Babylon plundered the temple, the ark was removed by Jeremiah and some priest. Then it was buried in a cave so no one could find it (Jeremiah 3:16).

God's Word indicates that the Ark and the Golden Mercy Seat are missing from the time of the Babylonian invasion and destruction of the first Jewish temple. Since the Babylonians didn't take the Ark into their country they did not suffer like the Philistines did. After Babylon, the ark is not mentioned to be in the second temple or in the list of things returned to the temple (Ezra 1:7-11, Ezra 5:14-15, Ezra 6:5).

Similar to second temple, the next Jewish temple will probably not have the original Ark of the Covenant. It will have a void holy place which the Antichrist will defile (Matthew 24:15, Mark 13:14, Daniel 12:10-11). If the Ark was there, then it seems that it would be mentioned in the Bible. If there is an ark in the next temple it will probably be a powerless replica.

118) What does the fig tree represent?

Now we will get into the prophetic portion of this chapter. The book Deep Foundations gets deep into the prophetic portion of the Bible in section 4. To start to understand prophecy and current events, we need to understand that the fig tree is a symbol for Israel's temple, not Israel. The nation of Israel is symbolized by the vineyard (Isaiah 5:3-7, Matthew 21:33-40) not the fig tree. The fig tree was rejected for a lack of fruit between the two final temple cleansings (Matthew 21:12-20, Mark 11:12-17). The fruitless fig tree revealed the temple's condition. Unfruitfulness is the reason God removed His blessing from the fig tree as well as the temple (Luke 13:6-9). Just as in this parable Jesus came to the temple (fig tree) for Passover 4 times during His 3 ½ year ministry. On His final Passover the fig tree's time was up (Matthew 21:19). This was a demonstration of God removing His blessing from the temple, resulting in the temple's destruction and removal (Matthew 21:20, Mark 11:20-21). Of all the signs of Jesus' return, the one Jesus focused on was the fig tree "behold the fig tree." Jesus revealed that the fig tree (temple) as well as many other religions ("and all the trees") would be back and flourishing before His return (Luke 21:29-32, Matthew 24:32-34). According to many passages in the Bible, the fig tree represents the Jewish temple, which is the heart and core of Judaism. Jesus focused on the Jewish temple's return as a sign that the last generation was here (Mark 13:28-30).

119) In the Bible 40 is often a *transitional* number.

It was 40 years between Jesus' death in 30 AD and the temple's destruction in 70 AD. During Noah's flood it rained 40 days and 40 nights (Genesis 7:12). Jesus was 40 days and 40 nights in the wilderness before starting His ministry (Mark 1:13). Israel wandered in the wilderness 40 years (Numbers 32:13).

120) A prophetic generation's timeframe is how many years?

120 years (Genesis 6:3). The fourth 120-year generation in Genesis 15:16 would be the people living between the years 360 and 480. This timeframe started when God made a covenant with Abraham. The end of the third prophetic generation is 360 (3 X 120=360). The end of the fourth prophetic generation is 480 (4 X 120=480). Israel left Egypt to head for the Promise Land in the year 430 (Exodus 12:40-41 KJV). This would be in the last ½ of the fourth 120-year Prophetic Generation. The God given number of 120 is the only biblical number that can be used to identify a

Prophetic Generation. The God given number of 120 is the only number that is consistent with every scripture. The popular numbers of 40, 70 and 100 fall far short of Israel's fourth generation entering the Promise Land. Therefore they are inconsistent with God's Word regarding a prophetic generation.

Genesis 15:13 is a little confusing, but there is an explanation that is consistent with all of the Scriptures. First we need to understand the Hebrew word עָנָה (ʿanah) translated here as afflict. According to the Strong's Lexicon, this word H6031 has a root word which is to speak. This Hebrew word ʿanah can be interpreted as evil speaking, resulting in humbling someone which can lead to abusing someone. It is not automatically saying to enslave someone, but can result in enslavement. The 400 year time-clock in Genesis 15:13 started 30 years later with evil speaking and mocking of Isaac by Ishmael (Genesis 21:8-9). The English word weaned is translated from the Hebrew word גָּמַל (gamal). A definition of the Hebrew word gamal (Strong's H1580) is "to deal fully with, recompense, also to ripen, mature or reward." When applied to a child, gamal covers the whole period of nursing and care until the weaning is complete. This period in ancient Israel could take years. When it was finished the child was mature enough to be entrusted to strangers or begin schooling. The completion of this period marked the end of the most vulnerable stage of the child's life, and it was celebrated with a feast. Isaac was the child of promise and the forefather of those who would fulfill the prophecy (Genesis 21:10, 12). The day Isaac was declared the child of promise was the day that started this 400-year time-clock. It began the time of Abraham's "seed" experiencing conflict and blessing while wondering as a foreigner. The 400-year timeframe ended when Moses delivered Israel from slavery (Genesis 15:14, Exodus 2:24). Moses had spent 40 years transitioning from an Egyptson prince to a shepherd God could use (Acts 7:30-31, Exodus 3:1-10). It was the Holy Spirit in the fire that was on "Holy Ground." The Holy Spirit came down to call and empower Moses to deliver Israel from Egypt to the promised land. The 400 year time frame and Genesis 15:14 was fulfilled 430 years after the Covenant God made with Abraham. Steven quotes this statement in Acts 7:6 which makes many assume, as Steven may have, that Israel was slaves in Egypt 400 years. This adds to the confusion but that assumption contradicts Galatians 3:17 as well as the Genesis genealogy. The phrase "entreat them evil G2559" is the same Greek word use twice in Acts 14:2 "made G2559 their minds evil affected G2559." which as in Isaac's and Israel's case started with mental abuse, which lead to prejudice and physical abuse. To understand the 400-year timeframe and these Hebrew and Greek words we need to look at this whole statement in the context of the whole Bible. When we do so we see everything mentioned in this answer adds up and also reveals God sovereign plan for both Israel's deliverance and which generation will enter the promise land. We also see God's sovereign plan is big enough to include our free will to reject it. We also see rejecting God's Word and plan has negative consequences. We also see that when the last generation starts God has a 120 year timeframe to prepare his church (Ephesians 5:27) and find a people that understands and obeys His Word. When that happens we will see churches preaching Jesus' words in Matthew 12:40 instead of religious traditions Mark 7:13. There will be one salvation message without the extra religious works (Ephesians 2:8-9) or teaching that God predestined us to go to Heaven or Hell (John 1:9, John 3:16, 2-Peter 3:9). Then Jesus' prayer in John 17:17,20-21 will be answered. I refer to this time as the next Great Awakening. The time chart at the end of chapter 6 in the main book Deep Foundations makes the 120, the 400 and the 430 year timeframes easy to see.

(Editorial note: Timeframe is a legitimate spelling that I use to pronounce this as 1 word instead of the 2 separate words, time frame. "The Cambridge Dictionary highlights both variations as correct by saying also timeframe or time-frame.").

121) **Did God predict which generation would occupy the Promised Land?**

Yes, the 4th generation (Genesis 15:16)

122) **How many years are there between Abraham's covenant and Israel coming out of Egypt?**

Exactly 430 years (Galatians 3:17-18, Exodus 12:40-41 KJV)

123} After Israel left Egypt, how many years were they in the wilderness?

40 years (Joshua 5:6, Exodus 16:35)

124} What is the total number of years between Abraham's covenant of promise and Israel entering the Promise Land?

470 Years /430+40=470 / 430 years between Abraham's covenant and Moses at Mount Sinai (Galatians 3:17-18) add 40 years wandering in wilderness (Joshua 5:6) equals 470. 10 years before the end of the 4th prophetic generation.

125} How long was Israel actually in Egypt?

Israel was in Egypt half of the 430 years. According to the Genesis genealogy, Israel was in Egypt 215 years. If you read chapter 6 in the book Deep Foundations you will see evidence that Abraham was still 75 years old when the Abrahamic covenant was established. The 430 years started when Abraham was 75 years old (Galatians 3:17, Genesis 12:4-5). Isaac was born 25 years latter (Genesis 21:5). Jacob was born 60 years latter (Genesis 25:26). Jacob was 130 when he arrived in Egypt (Genesis 47:9). Simply add these numbers 25+60+130=215, to find the biblical total number of 215 years. Israel went into Egypt 215 years after the Abrahamic covenant. 215 years is ½ of the 430 years listed in Galatians 3:17. It was the last ½ of the 430 years that Israel was in Egypt. Therefore Israel was in Egypt exactly 215 years. For more than 80 of those 215 years they were blessed with the best of the land, because Joseph second to Pharaoh provided for their every need (Genesis 45:17-20 + Genesis 50:26 = Exodus 1:8-14).

126} Is the Passover on the same day of the year (Nisan 14) as the Abrahamic covenant?

Yes, Exodus 12:41 "the selfsame day" $_{KJV}$/ "to the very day" $_{NIV, NASB}$ / "on the very day" $_{MEV}$. / What day? It was on the day of the promise given to Abraham about their deliverance (Genesis 15:14). Actually The Abrahamic covenant was a 2 day event because in the middle of that time the sun went down (Genesis 15:12) which begins the next Jewish day. These 2 days Nissan 14 *and 15 were high Holy days (Numbers 28:16-17, Leviticus 33:3, Leviticus 23:5-6).*

127) Are there any biblical references that the Antichrist will build the next Jewish temple?

No, there are references to him occupying but not building the Jewish temple. The theory that the temple will be built after the rapture of the church, by the Antichrist, during the Great Tribulation is not found in the Bible. What can be found in the Bible is that the Jewish temple will be rebuilt and this will verify that the last prophetic (120-year) generation has started (Matthew 24:32-37).

128) What is one of the main points in the parable about five wise and five foolish virgins looking for the Lord's return (Matthew 25:1-13)?

One point of the parable is that the Lord returned later than expected, so be prepared and equipped to shine beyond our currant generation (Galatians 6:9). It is a false assumption to declare that all the prophecies for Jesus' return have been fulfilled because they have not. God has plenty of time on His calendar to fulfill every prophecy, but we have a limited amount of time to do our part to be a light of love and truth.

129) What are the 3 seasons we should consider to understand currant situations?

Sowing, Growing, and Reaping / seed-time, growth-time, and harvest-time: Knowing the season we are in will help us properly interpret the signs we see. The same sign will have a different meaning depending on the season. For instance, if this summer I visit Michigan and see storm clouds approaching (the sign of a whether change), I would expect rain not a blizzard (different seasons render different results from the same signs). In the same way God has seasons for events on His calendar (Ecclesiastes 3:1). If we are not in the last generation yet, then maybe we should be unifying in biblical truth and preparing for the next Great Awakening, instead of yielding to misconceptions and preparing for darkness to overtake the world (1-Thessalonians 5:4, Matthew 5:14-16).

130) Is our free will and God's sovereignty both described as being in harmony in the Bible?

Yes. This is clearly explained in chapter 6 of the textbook Deep Foundations. God predestinated the fourth generation to enter the promise land (Genesis 15:16). God guided the people of that generation to the place where they had to make a decision (Exodus 40:36-38). Most of the people chose (of their own freewill) to reject God's Word (Numbers 14:1-11). They did not trust God and (of their own freewill) rejected God's plan, This resulted in them dying in the wilderness (Numbers 14:27-30). Their children were also part of that fourth-prophetic generation and learned the lesson from their parent's mistake (Numbers 14:31-33). They decided (of their own freewill) to follow God's Word and fulfill Gods plan for them (Joshua 1:16-18). They learned from history and chose to enter the promise land, which fulfilled God's Word (Joshua 3:14-17). These people entered the Promised Land 470 years after the promise was given to Abraham, which was 10 years before the end of that fourth Prophetic 120-year Generation. This is a clear historic example of God's sovereignty and man's freewill working together. God's Word was fulfilled but only those that chose to follow God were able to enjoy the benefits.

131) What are some aspects of God's sovereignty?

God rules. No one rules over God. No one is greater or even close to God's wisdom or power (Isaiah 55:9)

132) How can our free will exist in God's sovereignty-designed plan for our life?

God established the boundaries and gave us time. God's grand plan is big enough to include every situation, because God is sovereign. We are NOT puppets set in a lifeless mechanical play, fulfilling our preprogrammed movements. God has created us with the power to make choices that will affect our destiny. God has prepared a Godless place which He calls the second death or the Lake of Fire, but we choose if we want to have a Godless future or not. God does not predestinate anyone to go to the Lake of Fire (2-Peter 3:9). God give us that choice (Joshua 24:14-15).

133) Why is our free-will important to understand?

We will be held accountable for our choices on Judgment Day (Deuteronomy 30:19, Hebrews 9:27, 2-Corinthians 5:10 Revelation 20:12). If our soul could not choose between good and evil or choose to receive God's plan for our life then Judgment day would be meaningless. Those extreme Calvinist that preach such things do not understand the difference between the soul and nature (Hebrews 4:12). In order for love to exist there needs to be a choice to love or not to love, as well as a choice of how we show love and to what degree to express our love.

Further discussion questions

134} **How would you summarize this chapter?**

135} **What do you think was the most important biblical explanation to remember?**

136} **What Bible verses were the most revealing or noteworthy to you?**

137} **Can you think of ways to apply this information to your daily life?**

CHAPTER 7
POWER FROM ON HIGH

138} **When did Jesus do His first miracle?**

When he was 30 years old after he was baptized and the Holy Spirit entered His body (Luke 3:21-23, Luke 4:14, John 2:11).

139} **What was Jesus' first miracle?**

Turning water to wine (John 2:1-11)

140} **How much wine did Jesus make for a wedding in the village of Cana?**

About 162 gallons of wine at three firkins apiece (John 2:6-7)

141} **Is wine in the Bible always an intoxicating beverage?**

This is controversial. Some say wine is always fermented just as water is always wet. The book Deep Foundations takes the position that wine is a shorter way of saying "fruit of the vine." The Bible seems to support this definition by referring to wine being found inside a cluster of grapes (Isaiah 65:8 KJV). The words wine and juice are interchangeable according to the biblical translators, which use both words to describe the same thing. Wine is generally fruit of the grape vine, which can be turned into alcohol. Did you ever consider that it is unfermented grape juice that comes out of a wine-press? Wine is not always referring to alcohol because the Bible also refers to the wine and wine-press of God's wrath, which is the fruit of the vine of rebellion being crushed and poured out (Revelation 14:18-19, Revelation 14:10).

142} **In considering whether or not to endorse or drink alcoholic beverages, what should be our primary consideration?**

We should consider how it affects others, as well as how it affects our witness and our judgment (Romans 14:13). I know a recovered alcoholic who would never offer his adult son an alcoholic beverage, but instead warned him of the dangers and how alcohol almost destroyed his own life. There are many Christians that have been, or are still involved with ministries like Celebrate Recovery and programs like Alcoholics Anonymous. Even non-Christians that attend those programs can personally testify of the dangers of alcohol. As spiritual leaders we should always consider the ramifications of our endorsements.

143} **Since Jesus is in Heaven how can we say that Jesus dwells in our heart?**

Jesus actually dwells in us by the power of His Holy Spirit (1-John 3:23-24) The Holy Spirit contains the Identity of God and is one with God the Creator and Savior. The Holy Spirit represents "God the Father" and "God the Son" in us.

144} **Did Jesus dwell in the hearts of Old Testament prophets?**

Yes - the "Spirit of Christ which was in them" (1-Peter 1:11), "spake as they were moved by the Holy Ghost" (2-Peter 1:21).

Notice that the "Spirit of Christ" is also called the "Holy Ghost" and in modern translations He is called the "Holy Spirit."

145} Did Jesus have 2 natures after Jesus was baptized?

Yes, Jesus had the Divine Nature (Holy Spirit), which He received at His baptism and He still had His human nature (human spirit), which He received at His conception. This is illustrated in chapter 5 (The Last Adam – The God Man) of the textbook Deep Foundations.

146} What empowered Jesus to enable him to start doing Miracles?

After the Holy Spirit descended on Jesus, He denied His human nature and obeyed His Divine Nature and started living a supernatural lifestyle (Luke 3:21-22). Before Jesus' ministry with miracles began, the Holy Spirit led Him into the wilderness to do battle with Satan in His private life (Luke 4:1-2). Jesus never sinned privately or publicly but before beginning His public ministry, He needed to defeat Satan privately (Luke 4:13-18). Jesus was anointed to start doing miracles after the Holy Spirit descended on Him (Acts 10:37-38).

147} Why didn't Jesus do any medicals during His first 29 years of life?

Before Jesus' ministry years He submitted to the authority and identity of His human nature and His human family (Luke 2:51-52). Before the Holy Spirit descended on Jesus, He accepted His human nature's identity and lived a perfect but natural life. Jesus did no miracles as a child (John 2:11), but was wise beyond His years (Luke 2:40-47).

148} When we become "born again" Christians do we receive and have the same Holy Spirit that Jesus had?

Yes, Jesus gave His empowering Spirit to us (John 20:21-22, Romans 8:9,11). The same Holy Spirit that empowered Jesus to do miracles is now available to empower His church (John 14:16-17, Acts 15:8-9, 1-Corinthians 12:12-13, Ephesians 4:11-13, Ephesians 5:26-27, John 17:20-23). (You might consider reading the previous 6 passages together nonstop to get the flow of God's biblical message regarding the church).

149) **Can we become a "born again" Christian by doing good works?**

No, salvation is a free gift that Jesus paid for. We cannot earn our salvation (Isaiah 64:6, Galatians 2:16, Ephesians 2:8-9, Romans 3:23, Romans 6:23). (You might consider reading the previous 5 passages together nonstop to get the flow of God's biblical message regarding the fact that our salvation is a gift that we do not deserve). The Bible is clear that we are unable to earn our salvation, nor are we able to purify ourselves to qualify for salvation. The only thing we can do is to stop rejecting God's Word and receive His gift of a New Nature (the Holy Spirit) in our heart, thus beginning the process of transformation.

150) **When you study the Bible, what are some important keys the Holy Spirit will apply for proper interpretation?**

First determine if the information is literal or a parable or a parallel. If it is a parable or parallel then look for the principals or point of the story. Also the Holy Spirit will help you to see the context and consider the time, the people and the purpose of the information. Understanding the context will reveal the proper prospective and application of the information (John 14:26).

151) **What does water baptism symbolize?**

It is an act of dedication and discipleship, because though baptism we identify ourselves with Jesus' death, burial and resurrection. We go down under the water as a symbol of us burying our old rebellious ways of the past. We rise up out of the water with a clean conscience and new commitment to be more like Christ (1-Peter 3:21). Water baptism is a symbol that we have chosen to identify with Christ, join His family, and live as His disciple (Romans 6:4).

152) **Are there more than one type of baptism?**

Yes, the Bible even refers to the doctrine of baptizes in the plural sense (Hebrews 6:2).

153} **Both Jesus and Paul were baptized and encouraged others to do so, but did Jesus or Paul include water baptism as being part of the salvation experience?**

No, (John 3:14-18, Romans 10:9-10).

154} **What does the Bible say is essential to our salvation?**

Having the Holy Spirit of Jesus in our heart is the only thing necessity for our salvation and eventual transformation (Romans 8:9, Romans 8:11, Romans 8:15, 2-Corinthians 1:21-22, Ephesians 1:12-14). If you read these verses together nonstop you can clearly see that according to the Bible, all we need is God's Holy Spirit dwelling in our heart to be saved. God's Holy Spirit is the seed of redemption that grows in our heart to qualify us to enter and enjoy God's perfect Heaven.

Further discussion questions

155} **How would you summarize this chapter?**

156} **What do you think was the most important biblical explanation to remember?**

157} **What Bible verses were the most revealing or noteworthy to you?**

158} **Can you think of ways to apply this information to your daily life?**

CHAPTER 8
HOW WAS JESUS TEMPTED?

159} **Is temptation sin?**

Temptation is not sin, but submitting to it is. Jesus never sinned but He was tempted (Hebrews 4:14-15)

160} **Why did Jesus sweat blood in the Garden of Gethsemane?**

Jesus' Soul was experiencing conflict between His two natures. The struggle was to turn from His human nature "not my will" and submit to the Divine Nature "Your will be done."

161} Was Jesus ever tempted with immorality, dishonesty, or anything corrupt?

No, Jesus is the Soul (Person) of God and is not attracted to evil (James 1:13).

162} Did Jesus experience temptation similar to the way we experience temptation?

Yes, (Hebrews 4:15) Jesus was tempted at all the same points (or sources) that we are, but not with the same activities. We all have different temptations, but they come from the same 3 sources.

163} What are the 3 sources where most temptations come from?

From the human nature influencing the heart, from Satan and his demonic realm, and from peer pressure.

164} What are the 3 weapons the Devil often uses to corrupt us?

The lust of the flesh, and the lust of the eyes, and the pride of life (1-John 2:16);
The Devil used these weapons on eve (Genesis 3:6).
Lust of the flesh: "good for food."
Lust of the eyes: "pleasing to the eyes."
Pride of life: "make one wise."
The Devil also used these weapons on Jesus (Luke 4:1-13).
Lust of the flesh: satisfy your hunger with a miracle.
Lust of the eyes: Devil "showed" Jesus the kingdoms of the world.
Pride of life: You can do anything, because you are too important to die.

165} What does Satan fuel all his weapons with to make them more effective?

Deception (John 8:44, Revelation 20:2-3)

166} **What is the antidote to both pride and depression?**

Focus on helping others (Philippians 2:3-4, 2-Corinthians 1:3-4)

167} **Do we have power over the satanic spirits?**

Yes (James 4:7, Luke 10:17-20)

168} **Does the Bible say God Categorizes sin?**

Yes, at judgment day God will judge some sins as worse than others (Matthew 11:22-24, Luke 18:9-14). Even the same sin will be judged differently according to the individuals motivation and understanding (1-Timothy 1:13). Things done out of an evil heart with evil intent will be judged more severally than things done from a week heart that was seduced into sin. Every sin is bad but some are more devastating than others. The most devastating sin for us is to reject the Holy Spirit of God, because by doing so we miss the opportunity to be perfected and go to heaven.

169} **If God categorizes sin, what is the worst sin in God's eyes?**

PRIDE is the 1ˢᵗ sin listed in Proverbs 6:16-19 as things God hates. In Proverbs 16:5 God calls a proud heart an abomination. Pride was the 1ˢᵗ sin, which resulted in Heaven being divided and Earth being corrupted (Isaiah 14:12-15, 1-Timothy 3:6)

Further discussion questions

170} **How would you summarize this chapter?**

171} **What do you think was the most important biblical explanation to remember?**

172} **What Bible verses were the most revealing or noteworthy to you?**

173} **Can you think of ways to apply this information to your daily life?**

CHAPTER 9
TIME OF CRUCIFIXION

174} **How many days and how many nights did Jesus say He would be in the tomb?**

3 days and 3 nights (Matthew 12:40). When days and nights are put together like this, it is a very specific term for 24 hour days. There is no other way to interpret this. The original Greek can only be translated as 3 days and 3 nights or 3 complete 24-hour days. To say anything less is to disagree with Jesus and the 4 Gospels.

175} **When does the Jewish 24-hour day start?**

The Jewish day starts in the evening as described in Genesis 1:5,8. First there is the night followed by the day and the evening concludes that day and begins the next day. We think of evening as only concluding a day, but in the Bible evening is often the beginning of the day. We need to remember that when considering the timing of the Last Supper and the Passover Feast.

God created the Solar Day on day 4 (Genesis 1:14-19). Currently in Alaska a Solar Day could last for months. The ice-age happened after Noah's Flood. Before the flood there was a H20 canopy that surrounded the Earth like our Ozone layer does now. This produced a Greenhouse effect around the Earth. Therefore the 6th Solar Day could have lasted for months with comfortable temperatures before the Sun went down to concluded it (Genesis 1:31).

176} **What is the time difference between the 2 clocks used in the 4 gospels?**

About 6 hours during Passover, because Passover is near the spring equinox, which means there was 6 hours before and after midnight. At the spring and fall equinoxes days and nights are equal so nights are 12 hours long and days are 12 hours long. Therefore Jesus's statement in John 11:9 must have been close to the spring equinox. We know that Passover is near the Spring equinox, therefore the 12 hour long day is accurate on both the Gentile clock (which John often used) and the Jewish clock.

177} **What 2 things did the Jewish people do on the final preparation day before the Passover?**

Faithful Jews removed the last of the leaven from their houses and at the end of that final Preparation Day the Passover Lambs were killed (Luke 22:7). These things were not done on the day of Passover, because Passover Day was a High Sabbath (John 19:31). There was to be no leaven in the house on the day of Passover, therefore by the end of the final Preparation Day all leaven was removed in order to begin the Passover without leaven (Exodus 12:18-20). That is why Preparation day was referred to by some as the 1st day of unleavened bread (Mark 14:12).

178} **On the Jewish calendar, what day does the High Sabbath of Passover always fall on?**

The 14th day (Leviticus 23:5, Numbers 9:1-5, Numbers 28:16) If circumstances prevented someone from celebrating the Passover, they were to observe the Passover on the 14th day of the following month (Numbers 9:10-11).

179} **On the Jewish calendar, what day does the Holy Feast of Unleavened Bread always fall on?**

The 15th day (Numbers 28:17, Leviticus 23:6) This was the day following the day of Passover. Both the 14th and the 15th days were special high holy days.

180} **What does the Passover feast commemorate?**

The death angel passing over the houses where the blood of the lamb was properly applied (Exodus 12:13-14).

181} **What does the Holy Feast of Unleavened Bread commemorate?**

Israel's freedom and exit from Egypt (Exodus 12:17, Numbers 33:3)

182} **Was Jesus' "Last Supper" on the same day as the Passover Supper?**

No, it was the day before Passover, which is called Preparation Day (John 13:1-2, John 18:28). The Last Supper was at the beginning of Preparation day, shortly after dark (Mark 14:17-18). Jesus came into Jerusalem on the 10th day which was Palm Sunday

(Exodus 12:3). Jesus was in Jerusalem being examined by the people and priest for 4 days (Exodus 12:6). The 4 days are Sunday, Monday, Tuesday and Wednesday. These 4 days are the 4 days before Passover. "And ye shall keep it __up until the fourteenth day__ of the same month." Until Thursday the 14th but not including Thursday which was the Passover. The forth day was the final Preparation Day. It began at sundown which would be our Tuesday night after 6 PM. It ended 24 hours latter at 6PM Wednesday. Jesus' final Preparation Day began with the Last Supper. The Last Supper was on Tuesday night which was the beginning of the Jewish Wednesday. Near the end of the Jewish Wednesday, the Jews killed the Passover Lambs: "and the whole assembly of the congregation of Israel shall kill it in the evening." Also Jesus died on the cross at that time. At the very end of Preparation Day, Jesus was put in the tomb.

Using the Jewish calendar and clock, Jesus came into Jerusalem on Sunday the 10th (Exodus 12:3). We refer to this as Palm Sunday because of triumphal entry. Also Jesus cleansed the temple that day. Monday 11th Jesus cursed the fig tree and cleansed the temple again. Tuesday 12th Jesus was anointed with expensive perfume for His burial and Judas agreed to betray Jesus. Wednesday 13th was the final Preparation Day. This Preparation Day began with the Last supper and ended with Jesus being put in the tomb. Using our calendar and clock the Last supper would be about 7 PM Tuesday evening. Then Jesus spent the night in the Garden of Gethsemane praying, while His disciples slept. While it was yet dark, Judas arrived with solders to take Jesus. Jesus was mocked, beaten and presented to the High Priest before daylight. At about 6 AM Pilate ordered Jesus to be crucified. At 9 AM Jesus was nailed to the cross. This was the time of the daily morning sacrifice. At 3 PM Jesus died which was the time to kill the Passover Lambs as well as the evening Sacrifice. Jesus was put in the tomb and a stone sealed the door at about 6 PM Wednesday, which was the end of the Jewish Preparation Day. Jesus' body spent 3 nights and 3 days in the tomb. On the Jewish calendar this would be Thursday night and Thursday day then Friday night and Friday day then Saturday night and Saturday day. After the completion of the 3 nights and 3 days Jesus rose from the dead at the beginning of the Jewish 1st day of the week.

On our clock and calendar, this would be a little after 6 PM our Saturday night (Matthew 12:40).

183} What does the Last Supper, which we call the Lord's Supper, commemorate?

The New Blood Covenant provided by Jesus Christ who is our Passover Lamb (1-Corinthians 11:24-26).

184} All 4 Gospels confirm that Jesus was nailed to the cross on what special day?

Preparation day. This was the last day of preparation for the Passover. (John 19:14, John 19:30-31, Mark 15:42-43, Luke 23:52-54, John 19:41-42, Matthew 27:62-66)

185} Jesus was nailed to the cross on what day of the week and what time of the day?

They put Jesus on the cross at 9 AM Wednesday morning. Wednesday (Preparation Day) at 6 AM was the trial (John 19:14) leading to the 9 AM crucifixion (Mark 15:25).

Reading these 2 verses in the NIV or the NLT you will find obvious contradictions. Jesus' trial could not be at noon (John 19:14$_{NIV,NLT}$) when they crucified Him at 9 AM (Mark 15:25$_{NIV,NLT}$). The NLT makes another glaring mistake in Mark 15:42$_{NLT}$ saying this was Friday. This contradicts their own translation of John 19:31$_{NLT}$. This is another reason why it is better to read a more accurate translation like the MEV, KJ or the NKJ.

186} How long did Jesus suffer on the cross?

Jesus was suffering on the cross for about 6 hours, from 9 AM to 3 PM (Mark 15:25, Luke 23:44-46), which was from 3 to 9. The KJ uses the original Greek language translated to English which reveal that Mark and Luke were using the Jewish time clock. The NIV and NLT translate these verses into our Gentile time clock. These translations add to the confusion about what the Bible has to say about crucifixion day because they are ½ right and ½ wrong resulting in contradictions that lead to confusion and darkness.

187) **Jesus said He would rise from the dead "in 3 days" (John 2:19) and "after 3 days" (Mark 8: 31). How could both of these statements be true?**

The Jewish day ends at sundown, thus the resurrection was after the third day (after sundown Saturday). The Gentile day ends at midnight, thus the resurrection was in three days or before midnight. Jesus gave us a 6-hour resurrection window of between 6:00 PM and 12:00 midnight. Passover is shortly after the Spring Equinox. At the time of the Equinox there is 12 hours of day and 12 hours of night. Midnight would be 6 hours after Sunset resulting in a 6 hour difference between the Jewish clock and the Gentile clock.

188) **What day did Jesus rise from the dead?**

*Jesus arose from the dead at the very beginning of Sunday Jewish time (Matthew 28:1KJ). First we need to remember that the Jewish Sabbath ends at sundown Saturday night. The second thing to realize is this same Greek word translated here as "dawn" is also translated as "drew on" in Luke 23:54. "And that day was the preparation, and the sabbath drew on." Therefor we know that this is not a reference to sunrise. Also the word translated as "toward" can also be translated as "into." According to the original language this verse could and should read: "In the end of the sabbath, as it began to **draw on into** the first day of the week, came Mary Magdalene and the other Mary to see the sepulcher." At the beginning of the 1st day of the week Mary Magdalene headed for the tomb but Jesus had already risen from the dead (Matthew 28:6). Jesus rose from the dead after 3 Jewish 24 hour days (Mark 8:31), and on the third gentile day (Mark 9:31KJ). If you read the NIV Bible they changed this verse to match Mark 8:31 "after three days." Although they still say "on the third day be raised to life" in Matthew 16:21, Matthew 20:19 and many other places. The Bible repeatedly emphasizes that Jesus' resurrection was after 3 days and on the third day, which was Saturday after sunset and before midnight (Mark 10:34, Matthew 17:23, Luke 9:22, Luke 18:33, Luke 24:7, Luke 24:21, Luke 24:46, Acts 10:40, 1-Corinthians 15:4). By putting all the scriptures together on this subject we can see that Jesus rose from the dead shortly after 6 PM Saturday. This was also the first hour of the first day of the week Jewish time. "As it **began** to **draw on into** the* first day of the week." This was said on Mary Magdalene's third trip to the tomb. She first went to the tomb by herself (John 20:1). The second time Mary came to the tomb was with Peter and John (John 20:2-8, John 20:11-16, Mark18:9). On the third trip to the tomb Mary Magdalene brought Jesus' mother Mary (Matthew 28:1$_{KJ}$). If you read chapter 10 "Resurrection Day" in the book Deep Foundations you will see every scripture on resurrection day put in order with the approximate time of the event.

189) How does the Devil keep many people from seeing and believing what Jesus said and did?

The Devil uses the stick (threaten), carrot (incentive) and blindfold (deception) systems to hide the truth. The deceiver makes it more profitable to not tell the truth (Matthew 28:12-15). The deceiver threatens people to keep them from telling the truth (Acts 4:16-18, Acts 13:44-45, Acts 13:49-50). Satan deceives people so they continue teaching and preaching traditions handed down from forefathers and previous religious teachers (Galatians 1:13-14, 1-Timothy 1:13) rather than God's written Word (Mark 7:7-9). This produces ignorance, confusion, deception and divisions (1-Corinthians 3:3, 1-Corinthians 1:10). Departing from the light of the truth of what the Bible actually says results in exchanging real faith for darkness and deception (2-Timothy 4:3-4, Romans 1:21-22, Romans 10:17). When there is no standard, false doctrines increase (Judges 17:6). Spiritually speaking, having a standard is not just having a Bible. Having a standard is having the proper understanding of God's Word which enables you to see the truth. It does not matter who you are, if you disagree with God's Word you will be identified with Satan and fall out of favor with Jesus (Matthew 16:21-23). Jesus still loved Peter, but Peter was attempting to lead others astray by rejecting God's Word. To reject God's Word is to reject Jesus. Jesus is the Word (John 1:1). It is Satan that promotes disagreement to God's Word (Revelation 12:9, Genesis 3:1-5, 2-Corinthians 11:3 Mark 8:31-33). In the end, Satan's path of deception leads to a loss of vision (2-Corinthians 4:4). Satan blinds everyone who rejects God's Word. For some this blindness may begin with just a lose of clarity in their vision. It doesn't matter where we are in life, if we submit to God's Word, it will set us free from Satanic deceptions (John 11:43-44, John

8:32). The key is to have an accurate translation of the Bible like the MEV, KJ or the NKJ and be willing to leave errors behind and embrace correction and instruction (3-John 1:4).

190} **How can we drive back the satanic blinding darkness in our world?**

Proclaim the light of truth found in God's Word (Acts 26:16-18, Acts 4:19-20, Matthew 5:14-16). This was Jesus prayer before going to the cross (John 17:17-23). Verse 22 says "the glory which thou gavest me I have given them; that they may be one, even as we are one." I looked up the Greek word for "glory" in the Strong's Lexicon. The first two definitions were a positive "opinion, judgment, view" followed by "splendor, brightness." This verse could read: the (opinion, judgment and view) which thou gavest me I have given them; that they may be one in (splendor, brightness) illuminating their world. In these 7 verses of John 17:17-23, Jesus prayed 4 times that we would be one, which is to be unified. 3 times He stated what we are to be unified in, which is the truth. The unity and synergy of biblical truth will be a witness to the world. The definition of the word synergy is: The combined power or value of a group of things or individuals when they are working together is greater than the total power achieved by each working separately. Jesus' followers are to come together and have the same "view, opinion, judgment" of God's Word. This will bring light and truth and dispel darkens and deception. God wants us to be unified in truth but diversified in the way we express the truth (Romans 12:4-5, 1-Corinthians 12:12-18). We are all learning and it is fine to express deeper biblical truths, but take the time to verify that they are in harmony with God's Word (1-John 4:1, 2-Corinthians 11:14). If we are not careful the deceiver can influence even Jesus' closest disciples (Matthew16:22-23, Luke 9:54-55). It is good to have different applications or styles of delivery as long as they do not contradict God's Word (Luke 9:49-50$_{KJ}$, Luke 7:33-34). The reason people become spiritually deaf and blind is because of rejecting or misunderstanding God's Word (Jeremiah 17:23, Ezekiel 12:2, Romans 1:21-22, Ephesians 2:2-3). It is the fallen human nature that darkens our heart and separates our soul from God and His Word (Ephesians 4:17-18, Ephesians 4:22, Ephesians 4:27). If we want to drive back the satanic blinding darkness in our world we need to start with ourselves (Matthew 7:1-5, Ephesians 4:23-24). Every day we need to denounce our deceitful old nature and put on the armor of God (Ephesians 6:11-17). After we have denied self (the Old Man) and taken up the cross (the New Man equipped in the armor of God) we will be prepared for victory in the battle against darkness. Then we can look for God's direction for that day (Matthew 16:24, Mark 8:34, Luke 9:23). This 3 step process is a daily thing. God's glory is on us when we shine and illuminate our world with the light of God's Word (Acts 26:18). Walking in truth is a process of taking one step at at time (Psalm 119:105). Every 8 verses in Psalm 119 begins with a Hebrew letter of their alphabet. NUN is the 14th letter and it also has a definition which is: "faithfulness and the reward for faithfulness." We need to be faithful to the truth if we want to walk in the light. If we are divided with views and opinions that are contrary to God's Word, then the result will be confusion, darkness and blindness, which is an inability to see the truth.

Further discussion questions

191} **How would you summarize this chapter?**

192} **What do you think was the most important biblical explanation to remember?**

193} **What Bible verses were the most revealing or noteworthy to you?**

194} **Can you think of ways to apply this information to your daily life?**

CHAPTER 10
RESURRECTION DAY

195} **Would the Pharisees call for crucifixions on the High Holy Days of Passover, which would be Thursday Passover Day or Friday, the Holy Feast of Unleavened Bread?**

No (Mark 14:1-2). They were High Holy Sabbaths and Jews were not to work on these days but instead focus on God and what He had done for them (Exodus 12:13-17, Numbers 33:3, Numbers 28:16-18, Leviticus 23:5-7).

196} **Why did they break the legs of the 2 people on the crosses next to Jesus?**

By breaking their legs they would suffocate and die sooner so they could be removed from the crosses before the High Holy Sabbaths began (John 19:30-31).

197} **Why did they not break the legs of Jesus?**

Jesus' legs were not broken because He was already dead (John 19:32-33), which fulfilled a prophecy that He would have no broken bones (Psalm 34:20). The Passover Lamb that represented Jesus also had no broken bones (Exodus 12:46). This represents the unbroken structural strength of God's plan of salvation.

198} **When did Jesus' 3-day and 3-night time clock start?**

Wednesday evening at the end of Preparation Day; more precisely it probably started at the transitional moment when Preparation Day ended and the Passover began, which is probably the moment the tomb was sealed (Luke 23:52-54)

199} **How did the women know where Jesus' tomb was?**

They were there when Jesus' body was placed in the tomb and at the time made plans to return and anoint the body with spices on Sunday morning (Luke 23:55-56).

200} **Why did the women decide to wait 3 days to embalm Jesus' body and memorialize His gravesite?**

They had to wait to do this memorial service until after the Passover (day 1) and after the Feast of Unleavened Bread (day 2) and after the weekly Sabbath (day 3) had passed.

201} **What is the time frame of Jesus' resurrection?**

Using the Gentile clock: Jesus predicted His resurrection would happen after 6:00 PM Saturday (Mark 8:31, Matthew 27:63) but no later than 12:00 midnight (John 2:19-21, Matthew 20:19, Mark 15:29, Mark 9:31ₖⱼ). Jesus' resurrection was discovered soon after the third day had concluded, at the beginning or dawn of Sunday, the first day of the week Jewish time (Matthew 28:1). This verse is explained in question 188 but because of its importance in understanding the timing of Jesus' resurrection and the consistency of God's Word, it is repeated here. The Greek word translated here as "dawn" is also translated as "drew on" in Luke 23:54. "And that day was the preparation, and the sabbath drew on." Therefor we know that this is not a reference to sunrise. Also the word translated as "toward" can also be translated as "into." According to the original language this verse could and should read: "In the end of the sabbath, as it began to **draw on into** the first day of the week, came Mary Magdalene and the other Mary to see the sepulcher." At the beginning of the 1st day of the week Mary Magdalene headed for the tomb but Jesus had already risen from the dead (Matthew 28:6). Jesus rose from the dead after·3 Jewish 24 hour days (Mark 8:31), and on the third gentile day (Mark 9:31$_{KJ}$). If you read the NIV Bible they changed this verse to match Mark 8:31 "after three days." Although they still say "on the third day be raised to life" in Matthew 16:21, Matthew 20:19 and many other places. The Bible repeatedly emphasizes that Jesus' resurrection was after 3 days and on the third day, which was Saturday after sunset and before midnight (Mark 10:34, Matthew 17:23, Luke 9:22, Luke 18:33, Luke 24:7, Luke 24:21, Luke 24:46, Acts 10:40, 1-Corinthians 15:4). By putting all the scriptures together on this subject we can see that Jesus rose from the dead shortly after 6 PM Saturday. This was also the first hour of the first day of the week Jewish time. "As it **began** to **draw on into** the first day of the week." This was said on Mary Magdalene's third trip to the tomb. She first went to the tomb by herself (John 20:1). The second time Mary came to the tomb was with Peter and John (John 20:2-8, John 20:11-16, Mark18:9). On the third trip to the tomb Mary Magdalene brought Jesus' mother Mary (Matthew 28:1$_{KJ}$). According to the many events recorded in the Bible, Jesus' resurrection must have taken place immediately after the conclusion of the third 12-hour night followed by the third 12-hour day. This would be shortly after 6 PM Saturday. Many of the events immediately after the resurrection are recorded in the conversation of Luke 24:13-24, which happened on Saturday (Gentile-time) before midnight. We know this conversation happened before midnight because it was still "the third day" after the crucifixion and burial. The men talking with Jesus made this clear when they said: "today is the third day since these things were done." These things were done on Wednesday, so 3 days since Wednesday would include Thursday day 1, Friday day 2, and "the third day since these things were done" would be Saturday before midnight. Many don't take the Bible literally because they are confused about these things, but understanding how everything fits should increase you faith in the inerrancy and integrity of God's Word (Romans 10:17).

202} **Who was the first person to see the resurrected Christ and His empty tomb?**

Mary Magdalene (John 20:1, Mark 16:9)

203} **What did this person do after seeing the empty tomb?**

Shocked at the sight of the open tomb and missing body, she immediately turned and ran back to the upper room tell Peter and John (John 20:2).

204} **Did Mary Magdalene see Jesus the first time she went to the tomb?**

No, it was the second time she went to the tomb after Peter and John left (John 20:10-16 NIV).

205} **What was the difference between when Mary Magdalene seen Jesus and latter when Mary Magdalene and Jesus' mother seen Jesus?**

Mary and Mary were able to touch Jesus, because He was back from Heaven (John 20:17, Matthew 28:9).

206} **By sunrise Sunday morning, how many times did Mary Magdalene go to Jesus' tomb?**

Mary Magdalene had been to the tomb at least 4 times. Once by herself, second with Peter and John, then with the other Mary, and then around sunrise with many other women who were bringing spices for Jesus' body.

207} **When did the disciples truly understand the scriptures regarding Jesus' crucifixion and resurrection?**

After Jesus breathed on them to receive the Holy Spirit (John 20:22, Luke 24:45, John 16:13).

208} When was the first time Peter saw the resurrected Christ?

At the evening of Resurrection Day in the upper room (John 20:19)

209} When was the second time Peter saw the resurrected Christ?

Eight days after Resurrection Day in the upper room (John 20:26)

210} What was the third time Peter seen the resurrected Christ?

Between Jesus' resurrection and His rapture, He appeared for the third time to Peter and some other disciples at the last campfire gathering by the Sea of Galilee (John 21:14). Peter and the disciples made their home base in Jerusalem (Acts 1:4, Acts 1:8, Acts 1:11-14) but also made a trip back to Galilee as Jesus forecasted (Matthew 28:7, Matthew 28:10, Mark 16:7). It was probably at this time that Peter brought his wife back with him (1-Corinthians 9:5) to experience Jesus' resection (Acts 1:9) and the birth of the church (Acts 2:41-47).

211} After Jesus' resurrection, how many days was He seen of people before He was raptured?

40 days (Acts 1:3), this left 10 days before the Holy Spirit appeared on day of Pentecost.

212} What was some of Jesus' last words of instruction to His disciples?

Ye shall receive power, after that the Holy Ghost is come upon you: and ye shall be witnesses unto me both in Jerusalem, and in all Judea, and in Samaria, and unto the uttermost part of the Earth (Acts 1:8). And He said unto them, Go ye into all the world, and preach the gospel to every creature (Mark 16:15).

213} What did the angels tell the people after they seen Jesus go up and vanish into the clouds?

Ye men of Galilee, why stand ye gazing up into heaven? This same Jesus that is taken up from you into heaven shall so come in like manner as ye have seen Him go into heaven (Acts 1:11).

Further discussion questions

214} **How would you summarize this chapter?**

215} **What do you think was the most important biblical explanation to remember?**

216} **What Bible verses were the most revealing or noteworthy to you?**

217} **Can you think of ways to apply this information to your daily life?**

CHAPTER 11
WHAT HAPPENED TO HELL?

218} **Before Jesus' death, where did everyone go when they died?**

To the center of the Earth in a place called Hell (Psalm 16:10) also called Sheol in Hebrew (the singular place of the departed souls). Jonah died and went to Hell (Sheol). Jonah started to pray in the fish's belly (Jonah 2:1) and finished his prayer in Hell (Jonah 2:2). The Hebrew word for Hell in Jonah 2:2 is Sheol, witch is in the belly or center of the Earth. Jonah died in the fish's belly and his soul went to Sheol, the singular place of the departed dead (Jonah 2:7).

219} **How was Hell different before Jesus' resurrection from the dead?**

Before Jesus' resurrection from the dead, Hell had at least two parts. One part was a place of torment, the other a place of comfort (Luke 16:19-26). Above the Hell Fire there was a place called Abraham's Bosom or paradise, which is where Lazarus was, as well as King David, Abraham and the Old Testament Saints. There were probably three parts to Hell, similar to the layers of an onion. This top layer referred to as paradise, no longer exists because Jesus paid for everyone's sins and set them free from this section of Hell (Psalm 16:10, Ephesians 4:8-9, Acts 2:31). Today those that receive salvation go directly to Heaven when they die (2-Corinthians 5:8-10) and those that reject God's path for salvation are on the road to Hell (Isaiah 5:11-14). Today, all of Hell is a place of bondage and torment. There is a place of darkness referred to as the abyss and the bottomless pit, probably at the center. Around that would be the gates of Hell Fire (Matthew 16:18), which is where the rich man was that Jesus mentioned to in Luke 16. Today Lazarus is in Heaven and this rich man is still suffering in Hell. The Bible is very clear that Hell is a real place and strongly warns us that we can and should avoid going there (Matthew 5:29-30, Matthew 18:8-9, Mark 9:43-48, Luke 16:22-28, 2-Peter 2:1-9, Luke 10:8-15, Revelations 20:14-15, Revelation 20:10).

220) Are the devils in charge of any part of Hell?

No, instead an eternity of bondage, torment and Hellfire is their destiny. Hell is their prison, not their glory or kingdom (Matthew 8:28-29, Jude 1:6, 2-Peter 2:4).

221) Is the Bottomless Pit a real place?

Yes, the Bible refers to the Bottomless Pit as a real place, just as the Bible refers to the Devil as real creature with a powerful deceptive influence (Revelation 20:1-3)

222) If the Bottomless Pit is a real place, what is it for?

It is a place of darkness and bondage (Jude 1:6) prepared to imprison the Satanic which are extremely wicked (Revelation 20:3,7)

223) If the bottomless pit is a real place, where is it now?

Down, within the gates of Hellfire (Ezekiel 26:20), Ezekiel 31:14b "The nether parts of the Earth, in the midst of the children of men, with them that go down to the Pit." Ezekiel 31:16a "I made the nations to shake at the sound of his fall, when I cast him down to Hell with them that descend into the Pit"(Revelation 20:1-3). The pit is not just the grave (Although the grave is a depiction of the Pit's isolation and separation). The Pit seems to be the lowest part of Hell and is able to confine powerful spiritual beings according to the Bible (2-Peter 2:4). Therefore it has dimensions beyond our 3 dimensional world.

224) Are there fallen angels in Hell now?

Yes (2 Peter 2:4, Jude 1:6, Revelation 9:1-11)

225) Can demons defy God's Word and defile things not given to them and become subject to the Holy Spirit of God sending them to Hell early?

Yes (Matthew 8:28-29, 2 Peter 2:4, Jude 1:6)

226) Did Jesus go to Heaven when He died?

No, The Bible states Jesus went to Hell for 3 days before He was resurrected from the dead (Acts 2:27,31).

227) What are the differences between being revived from the dead and being resurrected from the dead?

To be revived from the dead, means you would still be mortal and subject to death. To be resurrected from the dead means you are physically resurrected to a new dimension of life. A life that is fresh, wonderful and supernatural. It is eternal life, free from death and bondage.

228) How did Jesus respond to the man on the cross that acknowledged his sin and asked Jesus to remember him?

Luke 23:43 - "Jesus said unto him, verily I say unto thee, today shalt thou be with Me in paradise." Paradise was another name for the good section of Hell. Jesus would be in Hell's Paradise with this man no later than midnight that same day.

229) When did the Holy Spirit leave Jesus?

Holy Spirit left Jesus just before Jesus Died (Matthew 27:46). Many wrongly assume Jesus was saying the Father left him but the Father is omnipresent and cannot turn away, also Jesus spoke to the Father right after this statement (Luke 23:46). Jesus was acknowledging that the Holy Spirit had left Him and He was identified by his humanity as the spotless lamb, having a spotless *human nature, which He presented to the Father as he died (Luke 23:46).*

230) When did the Holy Spirit rejoin Jesus?

The Holy Spirit rejoined Jesus in Hell before midnight of the day Jesus died (Romans 8:11, 1-Peter 3:18-19). In verse 19 the statement "By which also he went" indicates that it was after the Holy Spirit rejoined Jesus that He went to the place where David, Abraham and all the redeemed were. Because Jesus the Spotless Lamb took our sins upon Him (Isaiah 53:6), He first went to the place of torment as if He was a sinner (Luke 16:24-25). There the Holy Spirit rejoined Jesus and enabled Him to cross the Gulf which no one else could cross (Luke 16:23,26, Romans 4:25KJV). The Bible seems to indicate that before Jesus was raised to where Abraham, David and the poor beggar was, He went to the lowest part of hell (1-Peter 3:19-20, Jude 1:6, 2-Peter 2:4).

Even if you dismiss the former statement, this following statement is undisputable if you believe the Bible. Jesus entered Hell's Parricide before midnight (Luke 23:43). After Jesus arrived, He proclaimed their sin debt was payed and they would be set free in 3 days (Romans 6:23, Matthew 27:52-53, Ephesians 4:8-10). I believe Jesus arose first from the Gates of Hell to Hell's parricide (Acts 13:37KJV, Acts 13:33KJV) but I know He arose again to go into Jerusalem (Luke 24:33-46, John 20:19-20).

231) Is there now a Paradise section of Hell which some may refer to as Purgatory?

No (Ephesians 4:8-9), "Therefore hell hath enlarged herself, and opened her mouth without measure:" Isaiah 5:14a.

232) Now, where does a Christian go after they die and why?

They go directly to Heaven because Jesus has already paid for there sins (2-Corinthians 5:8). The Old Testament saints had to wait and look forward for Christ to pay for their sins. That historical event took place during Passover week in 30 AD. Now we look back to the fact that Jesus has already paid for our sins and made a way for us to go to Heaven when He hung on the cross and died for us (1-Peter 1:18-19).

233} What is the fate of those that reject God's biblical plan of salvation?

There are special books in Heaven (Revelation 20:12). If you reject God's plan of salvation, your name will not be recorded in the Book of Eternal Life (Philippians 4:3, Revelation 13:7-8, Revelation 21:27). Everyone not recorded in the Lamb's Book of Life will experience the second death (Revelation 20:14). Their names are blotted out of the book of mortal life because they never overcame their fallen nature and remained stiff-necked against God's Word (Revelation 3:5). They are spiritually dead and they will be buried in the Lake of Fire (Revelation 20:15). You are an eternal being, so you will not cease to exist. Therefore the second death is a reference to being separated from the population of Heaven (Isaiah 66:22-24, Mark 9:43-48). There are only 2 destinations for an eternal soul. Every soul will end up with either Christ (in Heaven) or the Antichrist (in the Lake of Fire); it is our choice (Matthew 12:30, Joshua 24:15). Before entering the Lake of Fire, those that reject Christ will have their lives exposed and judged (Mark 4:22, Revelation 20:11-13). Before judgment, the dead will be held in the center of the Earth in a place called Hell (Luke 16:22-28). When we die and before the dead go the Hell they will have an out-of-body experience where they are set free from their mortality (2-Corinthians 5:1-4). This is a temporary transitional time and some have returned to inhabit their mortal body and proclaimed that life does not end with death, even for the unsaved. This temporary euphoric experience does not change the fact that all those that reject God's plan for their salvation will eventually end up in the Lake of Fire as their final eternal destination (Revelation 20:10, Matthew 25:41, Revelation 20:15). The reasons for the Lake of Fire are addressed at the end of chapter 17 of the book Deep Foundations and will be discussed in questions 368 and 369.

Further discussion questions

234} How would you summarize this chapter?

235} What do you think was the most important biblical explanation to remember?

236} **What Bible verses were the most revealing or noteworthy to you?**

237} **Can you think of ways to apply this information to your daily life?**

CHAPTER 12
THE KEY TO HEAVEN

238} **Can you get to Heaven if you smoke, abuse drugs and alcohol, or live an immoral lifestyle?**

Yes sinners go to Heaven because Christ died for our sins and offers us a home in Heaven as a free gift (John 3:16-17, Ephesians 2:8-9, Romans 3:28).

239} **Will a proper acting agnostic be allowed into Heaven because of their many good works?**

No (Hebrews 11:6, Acts 13:38-39) There is only one sin that will keep a person from Heaven. It begins with rejecting Jesus and ends with blaspheming His free gift (Matthew 12:31-32, Mark 3:28-29, Luke 12:8-10). The unpardonable sin is to die believing the Holy Spirit is unreal, unnecessary or somehow evil, which is blasphemy. We cannot be saved if we die without personally receiving Jesus' free gift of His Holy Spirit (Roman 8:9, Ephesians 1:13-14, Romans 8:11, Romans 8:15-23).

240} **What is the purpose of the 10 commandments and the law of good works?**

To show us we are not perfect (Romans 3:19-20). It also gives us a standard to know good and evil (Romans 7:7).

241} **Who prepares our place in Heaven?**

Jesus (John 14:2)

242} **Who prepares us to be able to take our place in Heaven?**

Holy Spirit (Romans 8:1); we are saved because we first believe God's Word and then we are personally sanctified by the Holy Spirit (2-Thessalonians 2:13). Before we were created God chose this method for or salvation and sanctification. It is the Holy Spirit that gives us a new identity and makes us a new creation (Ephesians 1:13-14, 1-Corinthians 6:19-20, Ephesians 4:22-24, 2-Corinthians 5:17). It is the Holy Spirit that enables us to become God's children (Romans 8:9) and take our place in Heaven as members of God's royal family (Romans 8:11, Romans 8:18-19).

243} **In what part of Heaven will we have a home?**

The capital city, which is called the Father's House and New Jerusalem (John 14:2, Revelation 21:2-3)

244} **Do we have a freewill to choose whether or not we go the Heaven, or is it all in God's choosing who will be saved?**

Our soul can choose to receive or reject God's gift of salvation (John 3:15-18, Romans 10:9-13, Hebrews 10:39). God wants us, enables us, and encourages us all to choose life, but God won't make us choose life (2-Peter 3:9, Deuteronomy 30:19, Joshua 24:15). It is like a wedding, where the bridegroom initiates the process by courting the bride to be and then asks her to marry him. She then has an opportunity to respond with yes or no. If she says no then the man may continue to court her and latter ask again. If she says yes, they prepare for the wedding (Revelation 19:7-9). If she continues to say no, they will eventually part ways and she will not become part of his family. The Bible is clear that God initiates the process for our salvation and paid the price for our redemption. Likewise the Bible is also clear that God gives everyone the opportunity to receive or reject His free gift of salvation. In chapter 17 of the book Deep Foundations we will see that there are no exceptions, every human soul will have an opportunity to receive God's gift of life before the final Judgment Day. On judgment day we will be held accountable for our decision if we choose to reject God.

245} **In the Bible, what does the phrase the "Old Man" represent?**

The Old Man is a reference to the fallen human nature, which is often referred to as the Flesh (Ephesians 2:2-3, Ephesians 4:17-22, Colossians 3:6-9, Romans 8:8-9).

246) **What does the Calvinistic doctrine of total depravity and being dead in sin apply to?**

This doctrine applies to our human nature, which is often referred to as the "Old Man" or the "Flesh" (Romans 8:5-9). The fleshly nature cannot change (Romans 8:7). "It is not subject to the law of God, NEITHER INDEED CAN BE." The fleshly nature will always promote carnal thinking that will blind and corrupt the heart. We cannot please God when we are controlled by our fleshly nature (Romans 8:8). The word flesh here is a reference to our human nature not our human body because we can please God in our body (1-Corinthians 6:19-20, Romans 12:1). The Flesh, which is identified as the Old Man is totally depraved and eternally dead in sin. The Old Man will never stop its corrupting influence; therefore it needs to be replaced (Ephesians 4:17-24).

247) **Who is the father of corrupted mankind or more specifically the "Old Man"?**

The Devil (John 8:41-44)

248) **Does the "Old Man" ever get redeemed or regenerated?**

No, the corrupted human nature referred to as the Old Man is never redeemed. It is never regenerated. It never changes. It will never stop rejecting God's plan for our life. Therefore we need to cut off the Old Man's influence over our heart. The Bible refers to this as the circumcision of the heart (Acts 7:51, Deuteronomy 10:16, Jeremiah 4:4), which will be permanently done at the Judgment seat of Christ (Deuteronomy 30:6, Romans 2:29). We have to restrict the Old Man's power over our life by daily putting the Old Man on the cross (Romans 6:6). The Bible refers to this as taking up our cross and crucifying our self (Matthew 16:24, Matthew 10:38, Luke 9:23, Luke 14:27, Galatians 2:20, Galatians 6:14, Colossians 3:8-10). The flesh has to be removed not redeemed (Colossians 2:11). The Old Man will be permanently removed from us at the Judgment Seat of Christ before the wedding feast of the Lamb (2-Corinthians 5:10, Matthew 22:2-13, Psalm 103:12, Revelation 19:7-9).

249) **Do people that have not heard the name of Jesus have an opportunity to be saved?**

Our Creator gives everyone an opportunity to be His friend. It starts with realizing that creation has a Creator then trusting in the light God provides (Titus 2:11, John 1:9, Romans 1:19-22, John 12:35-36). There are many that die before reaching the age of accountability. They are too young or immature to realize we have a creator and savior. These people will go to be with Jesus during His Millennial Reign on Earth (Luke 18:15-16, 2-Samuel 12:23). They will mature during the 1000 year reign of Christ. At the end of that time all these people, as well as those born during that time will have a chance to choose between Jesus and Satan (Revelation 20:7-11). There are no automatic passes to Heaven. Everyone will have to make a choice. All the angels have already made their choice. All mankind will have an opportunity to choose between Jesus and Satan before the Great White Throne Judgment (Revelation 20:12-15). All those that were not judged at the Judgment Seat of Christ, will be judged at the Great White Throne Judgment, including fallen angels (Jude 1:6). After that judgment most will go to the Lake of Fire but some will be saved because they chose Jesus during the Great Tribulation or during His Millennial Reign on Earth (Revelation 13:7-9, Matthew 25:31-34). The people that enter the last millennium have their names written in the Book of Eternal Life. They will die at the end of the world and then they will be judged at the Great White Throne. They are rewarded for their good works with eternal rewards in the New Heaven and Earth (Revelation 20:12,15, Revelation 21:1-4). This is explained in more detail in "Section 4" in the book Deep Foundations.

250} Is there only one path to Heaven?

There is only one path that leads to Heaven, (Acts 4:12) Jesus has many titles and names (Yeshua, Messiah, the Light of the world) but all of them point to God the savior and the only path to Heaven (John 14:6).

251} What is the key to eternal life in Heaven?

The Holy Spirit of Jesus dwelling in our heart (Romans 8:9-11, Romans 8:15, Ephesians 1:13, John 14:26}. The Holy Spirit comes in the name of Jesus and represents Jesus in our hearts (1-John 5:11-12).

Can I lose eternal life or lose the key to Heaven once I have it?

Some believe eternal life is like a key that can be lost. There are verses that can be used to support that idea, which we will examine in order, to get the proper prospective, when we get to Chapter 16. The fear of loosing the key to eternal life often becomes a spiritual roller-coaster with up days and dark days of confusion, not knowing if all is lost. I don't recommend testing God and actively rebelling, cursing and rejecting God even in a moment of intense grief. However this roller-coaster concept, promoting the idea that we need to be good to qualify to keep eternal life is out of harmony with the Bible. The Bible has many warnings not to sin and encouragements to keep the faith, but the question is; if we are born-again can we be unborn? If I can lose eternal life do I actually have eternal life (John 5:24, John 10:28-30)? Eternal life is a gift from God that we can't earn and don't deserve (Ephesians 2:8-9). After God gives us the gift of eternal life (Romans 6:23), do we need to earn the right to keep it? If so then it sounds like God gave us a loan instead of a gift and if we quite paying the mortgage payments we lose our home in Heaven (1-Peter 1:3-4). The Bible indicates that God's children often do not act like God's children (1-Corinthians 3:1-3). You see everything changes if at any time we base our salvation on our ability to be good enough instead of God's ability to save us (John 3:16). There is a clear line in the Bible that defines whether you are saved or lost (John 3:3,7). That line between the lost and the save is, are you born-again? Just as our original birth is a one-time event that happened at a specific moment in time, our spiritual birth is a once in a lifetime event (John 3:5). We are not born-again of the Spirit because of our good works, but instead because we received God's free gift in our heart (Romans 8:15). The gift is a new nature, the Divine Nature making us part of God's family (2-Peter 1:3-4, Ephesians 1:13-14, Romans 8:9). Our old nature will continue to reject and blaspheme God and attempt to corrupt our soul (Romans 7:17-24) even after our soul has been born again into the family of God (Ephesians 4:17-32). Nevertheless our Old Nature has lost its ability to bring our soul to Hell (Philippians 1:6), because we are God's possession, bought and paid for (1-Corinthians 6:19-20). God dose not take back His gift when we yield to our old fallen human nature (1-

Peter 1:3-4). Our old nature will always and continually reject God (Romans 8:7-8). God understands that even the most rebellious child will eventually stand before Him in judgment and although that child will lose many rewards, they will still be saved (1-Corinthians 3:13-15). Both the good and the bad Christians are called to the Wedding Feast of the Lamb (Matthew 22:9-10). There is a judgment before the wedding (Judgment Seat of Christ) where Christians will be delivered from deception, corruption and rebellion because the Old Nature (Old Man) is removed at that time (Matthew 22:11-13, 2-Corinthians 5:10).

253) How do I personally receive eternal life and a home in Heaven?

We need to ask God into our heart (Luke 11:13, Romans 10:8-11)

Further discussion questions

254) How would you summarize this chapter?

255) What do you think was the most important biblical explanation to remember?

256) What Bible verses were the most revealing or noteworthy to you?

257) Can you think of ways to apply this information to your daily life?

CHAPTER 13
WHAT GOOD IS GOOD WORKS?

258) What are three different applications or types of faith mentioned in chapter 13 of the book Deep Foundations?

There is [1]*Saving Faith,* [2]*Perfecting Faith, which is the faith that produces spiritual growth, and there is also* [3]*Ministering Faith, which involves reaching out to others.*

259) If salvation is paid for and I can't earn it, then why bother doing good works?

Good works affect our quality of life both here and in eternity (Galatians 6:7-10).

260) **If a Christian backslides and becomes a disobedient and rebellious, what can that soul expect from God?**

As a child in need of discipline I can expect chastisement, not abandonment (Proverbs 3:11-12, Hebrews 12:6-8). Discipline is not always immediate. God hopes we will choose to repent from sin. God encourages us to be self-disciplined (1-Corinthians 11:31). By self-discipline I am referring to self-control, which is one of the fruit of the Spirit (Galatians 5:22-23 NKJV, NIV, MEV). The King James Version uses the word temperance in place of the phrase self-control, which most versions use. Temperance has to do with balance and abstinence which requires both self-control and wisdom.

261) **What determines the kind of harvest we will see from our actions?**

Ultimately it is God that determines the harvest (1-Corinthians 3:6-8), but we have a part in the process (1-Corinthians 4:2). From our perspective, there are 3 things that will determine the kind harvest we will see. They are the type of seed, the environment and the quality of the ground.

1) *Type of seed: The seed can be good or evil (Galatians 6:7-8, Matthew 12:35). The seed will produce after its own kind (Genesis 1:11-12), The seed may appear to be different from the harvest just as an acorn does not look like an oak tree which has the potential to become a forest. Our words are like seeds, which have the power to change the direction of our life, as well as others (Proverbs 18:21). We will give an account for how we use our words (Matthew 12:36-37).*

2) *Environment: Timing is a key element of the environment (Ecclesiastes 3:1). Just as the weather will affect crops, the environment impacts all seeds, but some seeds can change the environment (Mark 4:30-32, Matthew 5:14-16). When it comes to the spiritual seed of God's Word, we should always have it available and ready to plant (1-Peter 3:15, 2-Timothy 4:2-8). We should not be obnoxious about sharing the Bible, which tends to drive people away from*

God, but instead be sensitive to the Holy Spirit's guidance (Acts 16:6-10). Doing the Proper action at the proper time will impact our sowing seasons, growing seasons and harvest seasons (John 4:35-38, Galatians 6:9).

3) Quality of the ground: (Matthew 13:18-23).

262} Does the principle of sowing and reaping apply to everyone or just Christians?

This principal applies to everyone, saved and unsaved (Galatians 6:7). It can be either positive or negative (Galatians 6:8). It applies to many areas of our lives and is the key to the abundant life (2-Corinthians 9:6-11).

263} What are the contrasting objectives between Christ and Satan?

The work of Satan (the thief) is characterized by killing, stealing, and destroying; either directly or indirectly, the suffering in this world comes from previous seeds that matured in satanic gardens, sometimes three or more generations earlier, sometimes yesterday (John 10:10). Jesus stated that He will give us life (John 3:16-17, John 3:36, John 10:28) and abundance, supplying everything that is needed for our fulfillment (Philippians 4:19, John 14:6).

264} Why does God allow so much evil in our world?

God allows Satan a limited amount of time in order to provide the environment that gives us the freedom to choose between good and evil and understand the difference. These days of evil reveal that sowing evil seeds, not only affects us but also those around us as well as the entire environment (Romans 8:19-22). These days of evil will be a big contrast to Heaven, where there is no evil (Romans 8:18). This time of tribulation is an example for all eternity to see what happens when God's creation rebels against their creator. This time of tribulation reveals that you cannot reject perfection without becoming corrupted. You cannot reject the source of light, love and happiness without entering darkness and being consumed by bitterness and loneliness. You cannot reject the Price of Peace and the comforts of the Kingdom of God without being engulfed by regret and torment (John 15:4-6). There are only two options (Luke 11:23); you will either be with

Christ or the Antichrist. God has given us a CHOICE BETWEEN the freedom to enjoy GOOD things or the bondage of consuming EVIL. The more people choose evil, the more evil will dominate the environment like a virus and attempt to contaminate the good. Therefore God has made the Lake of Fire to isolate evil from contaminating Heaven.

265} What does it cost to be a true disciple of Christ?

To be Jesus' disciple we need to give up building our own personal kingdom and submit everything to Jesus' Lordship (Luke 14:27). Making Jesus our Lord is referred to as taking up our cross and following Jesus (Mark 8:34). If we read Matthew chapter 10 and keep everything in context we see Jesus is telling His followers of the power (Matthew 10:1,7-8), persecution (Matthew 10:16-28), and price (Matthew 10:34-39) of becoming His disciples. We can use Matthew 10:32 as a salvation verse because it is in harming with the Bible on receiving eternal life. However we can not use Matthew 10:33 as a verse to say we could lose our salvation because that is out of harmony with the Bible and out of context with this chapter. This chapter is talking about discipleship and in these two verses Jesus is pointing out the rewards to those that do not deny Him. Matthew 10:32-33 reveals the correlation between our actions here and our rewards or denial of rewards in Heaven. It is our rewards in Heaven that we have to work for, not our home in Heaven.

266} What is the difference between tithing and offerings?

The tithe is $10^\%$ of a Christian's income (Genesis 28:22, Genesis 14:18-30, Leviticus 27:30-32, Matthew 23:23). The tithe is not ours; it belongs to God. If we keep what belongs to God, He considers that stealing from Him (Malachi 3:8). Offerings come from the $90^\%$ of our income that is left after the tithe. We are to bring the tithe to God's church, after that we can give offerings, which God will bless. To refuse to give tithes and offerings rob God from the joy of blessing us. The tithe is considered the first fruits; therefor we cannot give God offerings until after we have tithed.

267} Is tithing $10^\%$ of every Christians' income a part of God's plan for the church today?

Yes, it was introduced in Genesis (before the law) and confirmed in the New Testament. Even Churches are to give of their income to help other ministries (1-Corinthians 16:1-3). As a Christian, a citizen of the kingdom of God, $10^{\%}$ of my income is for supporting the work of God at my church (Genesis 28:22, Malachi 3:10-12, Luke 11:42). Jesus said not to leave the tithing undone. Jesus is looking at the percentage more than the amount (Mark 12:41-44).

268} **How does giving generous offerings affect my life?**

It breaks the spirit of selfishness and draws us closer to God, resulting in God using us as a conduit to bless others (2-Corinthians 9:6-12). It is also a tangible way to multiply treasures both here on Earth (Philippians 4:19) and more importantly in Heaven (Matthew 6:19-21).

269} **Does sowing and reaping only apply to finances?**

No, there is much more to good works than sowing and reaping money or tangible things. The law of sowing and reaping also applies to our relationships and the ability to enjoy our life (Proverbs 18:24, Proverbs 6:14-15, Proverbs 11:17-19, Galatians 6:7-10).

270} **What does it mean to be a friend of God?**

Jesus is everyone's friend, but everyone is not a friend to Jesus (Zechariah 13:6, Matthew 26:47-50). Being a "friend of God" is a friendship where we are identified with Jesus and Jesus with us (John 17:20-23). This is a mutual friendship. It goes beyond just being children of God to actively proving that we love God and trust Jesus (James 2:21-23). God has many children, but not as many friends. To be a friend to God is a high honor. It is based on trust, obedience, and discipline (John 15:12-14).

Further discussion questions

271} **How would you summarize this chapter?**

272} **What do you think was the most important biblical explanation to remember?**

273} **What Bible verses were the most revealing or noteworthy to you?**

274} **Can you think of ways to apply this information to your daily life?**

CHAPTER 14
THE WAR WITHIN

275} **When and how do we receive the Divine Nature of God?**

We receive a new nature (the Nature of God) at salvation (Ephesians 1:13-14). When we ask to receive the Holy Ghost of Jesus into our heart (Luke 11:13), we then receive the new Nature as a seal of our salvation (2-Corinthians 1:21-22). In the Bible this new Nature is called the Divine Nature (2-Peter 1:4). When we receive the new Nature the Bible calls us a new man (Ephesians 4:22-24₍KJV₎). Both men and woman are referred to as a new man because the Bible is referring to our species not our gender (Galatians 3:28).

276} **What changes after we receive the Divine Nature of God into our life?**

The Divine Nature make us part of the family of God giving us a new identity and a new destiny (Romans 8:15-19). Here is a masculine reference calling Christians "sons of God." Earlier in this passage Christians are called "children of God." Both references include all Christians both male and female. Many times in the Bible masculine references like man (putting on the New Man) or sons of God are used to refer to identity and authority of the species, not the gender of the individual. God dose not want women to become masculine. Nor does He want men to become feminine even though the Bible uses a feminine reference for men and calls us part of the "Bride of Christ" (Revelation 19:7-8). The "Bride of Christ" consists of both men and women. It is use to illustrate our relationship to Christ as the head of the family. We know the phrase "Bride of Christ" is gender neutral because it is also use to describe Christ's home (Revelation 21:2, Revelation 21:9-10). God uses things that are gender specific to reveal concepts that are gender neutral. In the same way God uses things that are tangible (like trees and rivers) to symbolically represent spiritual things. Satan is the "author of confusion," but God does not want us to be confused about our gender or His plan for our life (1-Corinthians 14:33). When we receive the Divine Nature we become a new creation, a new creature, a new species, a child of God (2-Corinthians 5:17).

277) Does the sinful nature of man go away when we receive the Divine Nature of God?

No, Just as Satan did not go away when Jesus came to Earth, the old fallen human nature does not go away when we receive the new Divine Nature. If anything, the conflict becomes more apparent (Romans 7:15-23).

278) What are a couple of identities often associated with the sinful nature?

The Flesh (Romans 8:8) and Old Man (Romans 6:6). In chapter 14 of the book Deep Foundations is a diagram called "A Christian's 2 Natures" that reveals a complete list of identities of the sinful nature as well as the contrasting identities of the Divine Nature.

279) What are the 2 main sources of the thoughts or voices in our head?

(1) The sinful nature fathered by Satan. (2) The Holy Spirit who is the Divine Nature of God. The depiction of an angel on one shoulder and a demon on the other shoulder, both speaking to us, is not far from the truth. There are many voices around us speaking many things but they are also influenced by these same 2 sources (Proverbs 1:10, Mark 8:33, Acts 26:15-18).

280) Does both the saved and unsaved have these same two sources for the thoughts or voices in their head?

Yes, the human nature attempts to influence everyone, and God also speaks to everyone (John 1:9, Romans 1:19-22). There are many places in the Bible where God was speaking to people and through people but often God was ignored. If God didn't speak to the unsaved, no one would ever be saved. The Holy Spirit of Jesus is with us before He is in us (John 14:17, Revelation 3:20). Both the saved and the unsaved may refuse to listen to God and close their ears and shut their eyes to what God is saying (Acts 7:51, James 4:7-8); but if we have ears to hear and eyes to see, God will speak to us more often (John 16:12-14).

281} Spiritually speaking, can we identify the root by the fruit?

Yes, (Matthew 7:15-20). Jesus mentions the root of the fruit here. The good tree is the Divine Nature and the corrupt tree is the sinful Human Nature. They both bear fruit, but one is good and the other is always bad (Galatians 5:19-23). In many cases it is not obvious whether something is rooted in light or darkness. God will always lead us into truth (John 16:12-13). Satan is the master of deception. Therefore it may be difficult to see the root of the issue (1-John 4:1, 2-Corinthians 11:14-15). Satan will attempt to make bad things look good and he will also attempt to make good things look bad. Satan will plant bad seeds in our heart in an attempt to control our activity. For instance, is someone a thief after they steal something or before they steal something? They are a thief before they steal something, because an honest person would not steal anything, even when they have an opportunity. A thief is first a thief at heart before they commit the deed. Sin and deception takes root in the heart before the dark activity (Matthew 5:27-28). We should be slow to judge others but quick to judge ourselves (1-Corinthians 11:31) and not let darkness take root in our heart (1-John 2:9-11). We need to examine our heart (Luke 11:35, Proverbs 4:18-27). It is good to be aware of things we need to uproot and arias where we need to improve, but don't obsess over the negative darkness. Look for and focus on things rooted in love and truth until there is no room for hatred and darkness (Philippians 4:6-8). The best test to verify if we are in the light is are we or are we not obeying Jesus' main commandment (John 15:12, Mark 12:30-31, James 2:8).

282} How we can recognize whether it is the Divine Nature or the human nature planting thoughts in our heart?

If a voice (thought in our head) generally condemns us without encouraging us to do right, it is probably the Accuser (the sinful nature fathered by Satan). If a voice (thought in or head) points out a specific sin, indicating the need to repent and do something else, it is probably our friend the Counselor (the Divine Nature, the Holy Spirit). For some, the sinful nature will condemn and prompt shame and depression, but for others, or at other times, it will do the opposite and praise, in order to prompt pride (Psalm 36:2-4). Whether positive or negative the thoughts from sinful nature will promote darkness, deception and corruption (Mark 7:21-23, Matthew 12:33-35). The Holy Spirit will encourage and inspire us to do great things beyond our perceived ability (Judges 7:2,7, Judges 8:22-23, Hebrews 11:32-35, Philippians 4:11-13). Doing things with God prompts an attitude of gratitude instead of pride (1-Corinthians 15:57). It boils down to practicing the presence of God in everything we do (John 8:12). If we walk in the light, darkness has no power over us (Luke 10:19, Ephesians 5:8-16).

283) Do we need to Judge our thoughts to walk in victory?

Yes. We will be held accountable for the condition of our heart; therefore we should regularly judge ourselves and consider our motivations (1-Corinthians 11:31-32). We should maintain an attitude of gratitude for what Christ has done, is doing, and will do for us (Psalm 100:2-5). We should guard our heart against pride and presumption (Romans 12:3). We need to practice the presents of God in every aria of our life (John 15:4-5).

284) If I have bad thoughts, does that make me a bad person?

Our thoughts do influence our actions. That is why we need to guard our heart (Proverbs 4:23). Everyone has an occasional bad thought because of our human nature. We need to tear down bad imaginations, not identify with them or permit them to multiply (2-Corinthians 10:5). If we permit bad thoughts to multiply and take root they will make us a bad person (Luke 6:45, Mark 7:21-23), but we can repent and God will restore us (1-John 1:9).

285) Name something tangible the Bible uses to represent both the corrupted human nature and the Divine Nature?

Water: The Divine Nature, we know as the Holy Spirit is symbolized as living water (John 7:38-39, John 4:14). We can't live without water. Water is refreshing to the thirsty. It also provides cleansing from the unclean. In contrast the fallen nature is bitter water (James 3:10-12). The Bible also refers to these two natures as trees (Matthew 7:17-20). One tree has many branches of deception, corruption, bad theology and is rooted in sin. The other tree has many branches of truth, wisdom, good theology and is rooted in God.

286} What determines the kind of fruit we will bear?

Whether large or small, the identity of the fruit will come from the nature or root that fathers it. Our heart and soul will take on the characteristics and bear the fruit of the nature to which we are devoted (John 15:5, Galatians 5:19-23).

287} What does the biblical phrases in Matthew 16:24, to deny self and take up your cross, refer to?

Denying the fallen human nature from bearing fruit is to deny self. We do this when we identify with Christ and considering our Old Man (old identity) nailed to the cross and powerless over us (Romans 6:6-13). This perspective is how we becoming dead to selfishness and habitual sin (Romans 12:1-2). To go a little deeper into what it means to "take up your cross," it is to take up a <u>new identity</u>. We identify with Christ. We put on the "New Man" New Nature (Colossians 3:10) and apply the armor of God (Ephesians 6:11-13). When we take up our cross we are identified as "in Christ" (Ephesians 2:10, 2-Corinthians 5:17).

288} What is key to connecting to the Divine Nature?

The key to connecting to the Divine Nature is learning God's Word, so that we can recognize God's voice, know God's ways, and claim our new "in Christ" identity (2-Peter 1:3-4, Ephesians 4:22-24, Colossians 3:9-10). The "old man" is my natural human identity which is the combination of my soul and my fallen human nature. The "new man" is my new identity which is a child of God. I am a new creation (2-Corinthians 5:17) with a new identity and authority which becomes a reality when I am "born-again" (John 3:6-7, 1-Peter 1:22-23) of the Spirit. The "new man" is the combination of my soul (personality) and the Divine Nature of God which is the Holy Spirit.

289} If I am a new Christian or have backslidden into habitual sin, what 3 things should I do for growth and deliverance?

1) *Dedicate the body (Romans 12:1-2).*
2) *Purify the mind (2-Timothy 1:7, Ephesians 5:26).*
3) *Fellowship (Hebrews 10:25).*

290} How do I deal with shame?

The shameful identity is connected to the Old Man. We are not the Old Man. Instead we are a new creation in Christ (2-Corinthians 5:17, Ephesians 4:22-24). All the shameful fruit of the Old Man ends up in Heaven's graveyard, which is called the Lake of Fire (Matthew 7:19). All shame as well as our old identity is removed from the children of God (Romans 8:1, Psalm 103:12).

Further discussion questions

291} How would you summarize this chapter?

292} What do you think was the most important biblical explanation to remember?

293} What Bible verses were the most revealing or noteworthy to you?

294} Can you think of ways to apply this information to your daily life?

CHAPTER 15
WALKING IN THE LIGHT

295} Do we need to answer our critics and responding to the many accusations they launch against us.

Our focus needs to be on love not self-defense. We do not need to become sidetracked by answering our critics or responding to the many accusations authored by Satan (Nehemiah 6:3-16, Matthew 27:12-14). However, there are times when we need to explain ourselves in order to clear up confusion or remove ourselves from unnecessary abuse (Acts 22:25-30 – Acts 23 1-11). We don't want to lower ourselves to wrestling in the mud or becoming what we are accused of. We need to always focus on walking in God's peace and releasing God's light and love in every situation (Matthew 5:9-16).

296} **What is our best response to anyone attacking our Christian activity?**

Love and pray for them (Matthew 5:43-44, 2-Corinthians 5:18-20).

297} **What one word denotes the greatest and most universal commandment in the Bible?**

Love (Matthew 22:37-40, John 13:34-35, James 2:8).

298} **How important is agape?**

Anything done without love is done without God (1-John 4:8) and therefore not of eternal value to God's kingdom (1-Corinthians 13:1-3)

299} **What is tough love?**

Tough love is administering discipline, correction, or restriction in order to preserve or promote what is good (Proverbs 3:11-12).

300} **What is our key indicator that the Holy Spirit of God is in control of us?**

The key indicator is love (1-Peter 1:22), which means we have to have an attitude of forgiveness (Mark 11:25-26) or at least a willingness to let God start the process in our heart (Philippians 2:13). Without love, we cannot walk in the Spirit (1-John 4:16). Love is our key indicator that the Holy Spirit of God is in control of us and that we have His identity (John 13:34-35). Love is the main fruit of the Holy Spirit (Galatians 5:22). Without love, we cannot walk in the light of God (1-John 2:9-11) or be in harmony with the Holy Spirit. The Holy Spirit is called the Spirit of truth (John 14:15-17) therefore to be filled with the Spirit is to speak the truth in love as God reveals it to us (Ephesians 4:14-15). To love God is to love the truth (2-John 1:3-6) and hate deception (Proverbs 6:16-19).

301} **What 3 things are needed in order to actually reflect our new Christian identity?**

1) Reject the Old Man (fallen nature) from connecting to and enslaving our soul through confession and active repentance (Ephesians 4:17-32, Colossians 3:5-10).

[2] *Activate faith. See yourself in God and God in you. Know that the true reflection of God is Christ (John 17:20-23).*

[3] *Surrender all your personal rights to God and release God's Spirit to flow through you and from you. It's a cleansing force that will bear refreshing fruit. Not I that lives but Christ that lives in me and through me (Galatians 2:20). Christ did nothing except what the Father directed Him to do (John 8:28, John 5:19). Therefor Christ had the authority of God enforcing his every word (Luke 7:7-9). If we act and speak like we have supranational authority but are not under God's command or inline with God's Word or disconnection from God's Nature, we will find our words and actions lacing power and subject to demonic attack (Acts19:13-16). We are not to be a doormat and do nothing. We are called to be a light of truth and a warrior of God's kingdom (Matthew 5:14-16, 2-Timothy 2:2-4). I Can do all things in Christ (Philippians 4:13), I can't be in Christ and in self at the same time (Matthew 16:24, Mark 8:34, Luke 9:23). We can be Bold in Christ (Acts 4:8-19).*

302) If I decide to reject my Christian identity and act corruptly, deceptively, or immorally, would I lose my salvation?

No, The Spirit of God will always be within me because Jesus gave me His Spirit as a free gift when I asked Him to save me (1-John 4:13-15, Hebrews 13:5, Philippians 1:6). Once you are born-again into God's family you will always be His child. As His child you can choose to reject the Father's plan for your life, just as the Prodigal Son did (Luke 15:11-14). If you reject our Father in Heaven you will suffer for it (Luke 15:15-17). Nevertheless, like the Prodigal Son you will still be His child, even if you choose to live in a sinful lifestyle (Luke 15:18-24). Some may say that he was dead and lost and therefore not a son (Luke 15:19,21). The Bible states even when the Prodigal was considered a dead son (Luke 15:24) and lost brother (Luke 15:27) he was still a member of the family (Luke 15:17,30). As a children of God we can act like the spiritually dead and lose our fellowship with the Father, but if we return to connecting with God, then God will joyfully receive us (Luke 15:32). We can lose our inheritance (treasures in Heaven) because they are based on what we have done (Matthew 6:19-20). However, we will not lose our home in Heaven because it is based on what Jesus has done (John 14:2). We will go deeper into this subject in the next chapter.

303) **What 3 identities did the Apostle Paul claim, which identified him at different stages of his life?**

1) Saul (Acts 9:4)   *2) Paul (Acts 13:9)*   *3) In Christ (Galatians 2:20, Philippians 1:21)*

304) **What 3 stages of life did the Apostle Paul experience that is symbolized in the Old Testament?**

1) Egypt = The natural child born into the satanic world system full of bondage and corruption leading to death (Acts 8:1-3, Acts 9:1-5).
2) Wilderness = The born-again child of God destined for Heaven, yet still struggling with the slave to sin mindset (Romans 7:14-25).
3) Promised Land = The Spirit lead child of God enjoying the fruit of the Spirit, leading to a place of victory and peace (Philippians 4:11-13).

305) **What does the Bible say that it takes to be a true disciple of Christ?**

Deny self in order to properly follow Jesus and be faithful in praying and obeying, even if it will cost me my life. This means to consider my relationship to God far above any other relationship. We demonstrate this when there is a choice between following a loved one or God (Luke 14:26, Matthew 16:22-23). A true disciple needs to daily crucify self, which means to deny my selfish human nature (Galatians 2:20, Galatians 5:24). A true disciple needs to surrender all to God (Matthew 16:24, Luke 14:27). This means to give up my personal rights (Luke 14:33, Matthew 16:25). Dedicate time to meditating on God's word (John 8:31). Love others (John 13:35). This gives us the context to understand Luke 14:26. Everything is to be done in love but it should appear as if we hated anything that would come between us and God.

306) **What is the first reaction most people have when they realize what it takes to be a disciple of Christ?**

Just like the early Israelites, many Christians turn back after they first see the Promised Land (their "high calling"). They see the obstacles and consider the fruit unattainable (Numbers 13:27-33), or they attempt to attain the Promised Land by their own willpower (Numbers 14:40-45) instead of submitting to God's Word and depending on God's help (Numbers 13:23-30, Numbers 14:8-9).

307) What is the key to the Promised Land of victory over the circumstances?

The "in Christ" identity; it enables us to maintain an attitude of love, peace, and joy, in spite of any negative circumstances. To identify with Christ we first need to understand what it means to be "in Christ" and then act as an extension of Him (John 15:5). Then we can deal with the temporary circumstances with an eternal perspective (Hebrews 12:2). God supplies the light of hope and love that will vanquish the dark fears, frustrations and futility of the carnal life. Instead of hate and despair, we can choose to connect with God though prayer.

308) Can I opt out of the spiritual war that is now going on throughout this Earth?

This war affects us whether we realize it or not. It is the conflict between good and evil. The kingdom of God is in opposition to the realm of darkness. On one side there is love and truth, on the other, deception and corruption (Luke 11:23-26).

309) Can a Christian become a casualty in this spiritual war of the ages?

Some have died because of ignorance of God's word (2-Samuel 6:6-7, 1-Chronicles 15:2). Some have died because of disobedience to God's word (1-Corinthians 11:30-31). Some have committed suicide because of demonic oppression (John 10:10). Many have been on the front line and died as martyrs (Acts 7:52-60, Hebrews 11:33-37, Luke 23:46). The reality is that until the King of kings comes back, all will die because of the condition of this world (Hebrews 9:27). However, if you are equipped with the armor of God, Satan can't kill you until you have fulfilled your mission (Acts 28:3-10). The question is not will you be a casualty of this fallen world, but instead will you die faithful to God in this war of the ages (2-Timothy 4:6-8).

310) Can a Christian become enslaved by demons or end up as a prisoner of war?

Drugs, alcohol and witchcraft are doors to demonic deception, oppression and bondage (1-Peter 5:8). Yielding habitually to sin enables the demonic to use that sin to enslave us (Romans 6:16). Self-righteous pride is a demonic trap to separate us from God in order to defeat us (Proverbs 16:18, Luke 22:31-34) The greater the degree that these things are done, the greater the chance of becoming imprisoned by them, allowing Satan to use and abuse us (Ephesians 4:27).

311) If a Christian is in emotional bondage can they be set free, and if so, How?

First, focus on spending a lot of time meditating on God's Word (2-Peter 1:2-9). This will enable you to apply the helmet of salvation for access to the mind of Christ (1-Corinthians 2:12-16). Then we can see things though the eyes of Jesus and clear away the voices that drown out God's Word (Ephesians 4:22-32). After the helmet of salvation containing our new identity is firmly in place (Romans 12:2) put on the whole armor of God, that ye may be able to stand against the wiles of the Devil (Ephesians 6:10-13). After spending a significant amount of time in God's Word then focus on helping others (2-Corinthians 1:3-4, Philippians 2:2-5).

312) A Christian disciple is called to what two positions or job descriptions in order to fulfill the Great Commission?

1) We are called to be God's Ambassadors to the souls of this world. We are to love them and open the doors of freedom to them (2-Corinthians 5:20, Isaiah 42:7, Acts 26:18).
2) We are called to be Christ's Soldiers fighting against corruption. We are to fight against corruption and depravity, whether it comes from the fallen nature or the fallen angels (2-Timothy 2:3, Ephesians 6:11-13).

313) Where is the main Battlefield that both God and Satan desire to possess?

The main Battlefield is in the heart. The heart is the key to the redemption of a person and revival of a nation (Proverbs 4:23, Luke 6:45, Matthew 15:18-19).

314} What is our personal mission in order to weaken the enemy's strongholds throughout the battlefield?

Our mission is to plant the seeds of truth in the hearts of others and water them with love (2-Corinthians 10:3-5).

315} What should we evaluate before we focus on helping others?

Before we focus on others, we should evaluate our motivations and priorities. First cast the beam out of our own eye so that we can see clearly to help others (Luke 6:41-42). By removing the obstructions to the light, we allow God to shine through us in a powerful way (Matthew 6:22-24, Ephesians 5:8-11, Matthew 5:14-16).

316} What was the famous statement Jim Elliott wrote down that became a battle cry after he was killed?

"It is no fool to give up what he cannot keep to gain what he cannot lose."

Further discussion questions

317} How would you summarize this chapter?

318} What do you think was the most important biblical explanation to remember?

319} What Bible verses were the most revealing or noteworthy to you?

320} Can you think of ways to apply this information to your daily life?

CHAPTER 16
FROM CORRUPTION TO PERFECTION

321} Can a born-again Christian lose their salvation?

No, but some have misinterpreted a few scriptures and teach that gaining and retaining our salvation is base upon our good works and avoiding sins. The Bible states in many places that salvation is a matter of accepting what God has done for us, not God accepting what we have done for Him (John 14:6, Ephesians 2:1-9, Romans 6:23, John 3:16, Luke 11:13, John 14:16, Romans 8:15, Philippians 1:6). According to the Bible once you are born-again of the Spirit you have eternal life and cannot be unborn. A Christian may lose rewards for bad behavior, but he won't lose his gift of eternal life (1-Corinthians 3:15). Salvation is a gift from God, not a payment for our good works. Our good works cannot perfect us or prepare us to enter and be a part of a perfect place called Heaven. Only God's gift can prepare us for faultless perfection. This is because God's gift is a new pure and Holy Nature (the Divine Nature) that will replace our sinful nature (Ephesians 1:13-14, Luke 11:13, Ephesians 4:30, Romans 8:23, 2-Corinthians 1:21-22). This will transform our heart. In Heaven our heart will not receive information from our sinful nature because it will be removed (Romans 2:29, Colossians 2:11). Therefore our heart will only receive and provide information from the Divine Nature, or information that is filtered by the Holy Spirit. This will supply to the soul with better information because it comes from a completely different and perfected source. The Bible refers to this as a new heart. (Ezekiel 36:26-27, Ezekiel 11:19-20). Therefore in Heaven we will no longer have a sin-nature spreading corruption and deception. Instead we will only have the Divine Nature that magnifies and multiplies perfection, truth and love. Our Heavenly identity will be "in Christ" not "In Adam"(1-Corinthians 15:22, 2-Corinthians 5:17-21, Colossians 1:27-28). For more insights to the security of the believer, you can review the answer to question 252. The next 2 questions will reveal insights to understand the verses that seem to indicate that we can lose our salvation.

322} What is 1-Corinthians 3:16-17 referring to?

This passage is not talking about a man who smokes, overeats, gets drunk, or commits suicide. It is talking about the root of all those things – the Old Man. It is the Old Man (the old human nature) who defiles the temple. The Old Man is the source of our bad attitudes and actions (Ephesians 4:22). The old nature is the Old Man who defiles the temple of God, and "him shall God destroy."

323) What is Matthew 22:10-13 talking about?

This parable signifies that judgment will fall on the Old Man (human nature) before a special royal wedding (Revelation 19:6-9), and he will be removed at that time.

324) What is covered by the garment of righteousness provided by the King of kings?

The garment of righteousness covers our soul, not our fallen human nature (Isaiah 61:10).

325) Will Christians face judgment for the actions done during their lifetime on Earth?

Yes, Christians are judged at the Judgment Seat of Christ (2-Corinthians 5:10, Romans 14:12). At the Judgment Seat of Christ Christians will receive rewards or loss of rewards (1-Corinthians 3:11-15). Every word we speak we will give an account for on Judgment Day (Matthew 12:34-37). The Judgment Seat of Christ is where the Old Man is exposed, judged and removed (1-Corinthians 3:16-17, Matthew 22:10-13). The Judgment Seat of Christ occurs after the raptures and before the Wedding Feast of the Lamb.

326) Does Matthew 20:1-15 mean that everyone is the same in Heaven and will receive the same rewards?

Some may think that this parable indicates everyone will receive the same rewards, but that interpretation is out of harmony with many parts of the Bible. A better interpretation would be that both child salvations and deathbed confessions receive the same status as a child of God and will live in the same capital city in Heaven. This explanation is consistent with the entire Bible which declares all people, no matter their age or background, are welcome to join the family of God through faith and receive eternal life with Christ in Heaven (Galatians 3:28-29). Although this parable mentions wages, eternal life is not something we can earn or deserve (Ephesians 2:4-9). Eternal life is not a reword for *good works (Romans 3:22-24). Eternal life is a gift Christ paid for and offers freely to all (Romans 5:8-18). Although salvation is free, it is not automatic; we must respond to the call. If we respond to God's call, we will receive a benefit. This parable in Matthew 20:1-15 illustrates that the wage or benefit (salvation) is connected to responding to the call, not in the work that was done after the call. There may be other interpretations to this parable, but they must be in harmony with the Bible to be beneficial.*

327) Will some receive more awards and different rewards in Heaven because of good works done during their lifetime?

Yes, some will have more eternal treasures because they chose to invest part of their time, talent and treasure in the Kingdom of God (Matthew 6:20). Rewards will be given according to, and because of the works that were done and decisions that were made while living on Earth (Revelation 22:12).

328) Will a Christian's sins be covered up and never seen if they confess them to God and ask for forgiveness?

Some may not agree but the Bible states many times that nothing will be hid (Matthew 10:26). The good and bad will be seen (1-Corinthians 3:13-15) as well as the hidden root that motivated the actions (1-Corinthians 4:5). To some degree there are consequences for every sin. For instance, if I murder someone there is forgiveness but there are also consequences. David's life and great sin is recorded in the eternal Bible and is just one of many examples that nothing will be hid, but everything can be confessed and forgiven (1-John 1:9) and we can be reinstated as God's agent, just as Peter was (John 21:15-19).

329) When and how are our sins separated from us, as far as the east is from the west, never to be seen again?

At the Judgment seat of Christ (2-Corinthians 5:10) the good and bad are seen. This includes the things done with God as well as our sins (Luke 12:2-3). The Old Man will be exposed. Sin is separated from us when the Old Man is cast out (Matthew 22:10-13). Now as Christians we have the seed that will make us a new creation (Romans 8:9-23). After the Old Man is separated from us we will have no connection or identification with sin ever again

(Zephaniah 3:15, 2-Corinthians 5:17, Romans 8:1-2). This does not mean that the Old Man's history is erased but instead our connection to him is removed and we are a new creature that is forever identified as a Child of God and member of the perfect ruling class of Heaven. We are perfected and will never sin again. Just as an Eagle is not identified with an eggshell, we will never again be connected to or identified with the sinful Old Man (Isaiah 40:31).

330} Would God ever expose our past sins for all to see, and if so why?

There will be many wonderful rewards at the Judgment Seat of Christ, but this is also a time of exposing and purifying. It's kind of like opening a festering wound to release the poison. It is a time of clearing the air of misunderstandings and clearly seeing the whole picture of life's activities. Everything will be seen clearly, even the motives, influences, misunderstandings, and hidden things (Mark 4:22, 1-Corinthians 4:5). At that time, we will see everything, the good and the bad. We will not be proud. We will instead be humbly and eternally grateful to Jesus Christ for removing the sinful identity and making us a new creation. We will fully understand each other and ourselves. We will see and understand the root of division and conflict. Two Christians that were at war with each other will see the true enemy and unite against the Old Man. This is how they will be liberated from hate and united in love and restoration (1-Corinthians 13:12-13).

331} The book Deep Foundations list three applications of the parable listed in Matthew 13:24-30: Describe Two.

The First and primary Application of the parable the saved and the lost; There are only two classes of people in this world, the saved and the lost. This separation is literally performed at the end of this world. We see this in Revelation 20:9 through Revelation 21:4. There are only two eternal destinations. The saved and the lost will dwell together for now but every person will go to one of two places – either Heaven or the Lake of Fire.
The Second Application addresses the root (seeds) that distinguish the saved from the lost, which is the human nature and the Divine Nature. The entity that makes us "children of the kingdom" or "children of the Wicked One" is our nature. In the

wheat and tares parable, these two natures are identified as two different seeds that develop a different root system. The identity of the tares would be that which the Devil planted or what the Devil fathered. The seed of redemption was prepared to come forth before we had a problem, before the tares appeared (1-Peter 1:18-20). Redemption is receiving the Divine Nature of Jesus, which the "Word" of God (John 1:1) has made available to us. This implantation was foreordained to redeem our soul and make us a new creation (Ephesians 1:3-4). Redemption would start with the Seed of the Spirit being planted in our heart but would be a processes leading to perfection (Romans 8:22-23). God knew Satan would successfully sow seeds of corruption that would lead to death and destruction. Therefore, before He created mankind God chose how He would redeem mankind. God's predetermined plan of salvation would include a processes that would produce a new species referred to as the children of God. The soul has an option to allow transformation or resist it (Ephesians 5:26, Joshua 24:15, John 3:16-18, Romans 10:13, Romans 10:8-10, Luke 11:13). There are only 2 classes of people, the save and the lost, those that have the Spirit of Jesus in their hearts and those that do not (Romans 8:9, Luke 11:23). The seed gives the field its identity, just as the nature gives the soul its identity. We can go from the identity of a field of weeds choking out God's blessings to "good ground" for God's seed to bear precious fruit.

A Third application could be a reference to the spiritual war between light and darkness, truth and deception. In the end all deception will be removed and the light of truth will win. In the end the deceptive satanic forces of evil will be confined in the Lake of Fire.

332} Does God predestinate who will go to Heaven, and therefore also predestine who will go to Hell?

No, God is Not willing that any perish (2-Peter 3:9). God desires us to love and trust Him (Matthew 22:37). True love and trust cannot exist without the ability to choose. God's Word repeatedly states that we have a choice (Deuteronomy 30:19, Joshua 24:15, 2-Timothy 4:3-4, 2-Peter 2:21). Could God, who is a Righteous Judge (2-Timothy 4:8) condemn a man born blind, for not seeing, if he never had a chance to see the light? No, therefore God brings the light to every man (John 1:6-9). If anyone rejects the light of God in order to remain in darkness (John 3:19-20, Romans 1:19-22) then they will be held accountable for their choice. It is OUR CHOICES we will be held accountable for. It is our choice whether we go to Heaven or Hell (John 3:15-18, Deuteronomy 30:19). Extreme Calvinism takes a few scriptures out of their Biblical context and does not understand the difference between our soul which has a free will, and our totally depraved fallen nature (Hebrews 4:12), which never changes (Romans 8:7). Consequently it limits both God's ability to give us a choice and our ability to choose and therefore exalts fate over faith. Extreme Calvinism teaches that some are created and chosen for Heaven but is reluctant to admit that if that were true then God create some people to go to Hell. You can't have one without the other. They are the two sides of the same coin of election and the unelected. Extreme Calvinism turns God into a great puppet-master micromanaging every event. This is because this philosophy misunderstands God's sovereignty. God is Sovereign, which simply means God makes the rules and no one rules over God. God created the law of seed-time and harvest as well as the law of gravity. We are subject to the laws God established and if we violate the law there are natural consequences (Galatians 6:7). For example, if I jump out of an airplane, God does not have to push me down, the law of gravity (which was established long ago) will push me down. God created the law of gravity but He is not subject to gravity. Jesus proved this when He walked on the water (Matthew 14:25) and was raptured (Acts 1:9-11). God rules and establishes bounders but does not micromanage our every move. God restricts Satan's demonic activity, but does not micromanage Satan's every move (1-Peter 5:8, Ephesians 6:11-12). One day God will restrict Satan and all his demonic activity to the lake of fire (Revelation 20:10). But for now God uses Satan to give us a choice between the light of God's kingdom and the realm of darkness. We can choose to obey God or not. We can choose follow His rules and plan of salvation or not. The consequence of turning away from the light is we enter darkness.

333) What is a biblical definition of the word Predestinate?

The biblical word Predestinate has two parts to its definition:

- First – there would be a predetermined path of redemption. Our predetermined path for salvation according to Jesus is **"Ye must be born again"** (John 3:3,7). When we are born again we are then identified as "in Christ," and therefore members of God's family.
- Second – there would be a predesigned destination. Our predesigned destination is to be perfect like Christ (Ephesians 4:15-16) and have a special place in Heaven prepared specifically for us.

334} In what way are the redeemed predestinated?

The redeemed are predestinated to be conformed to the image of Christ. This means that we will be without corruption after we die. Our destiny is predetermined and prearranged to be without corruption. We are predestinated to perfection (Romans 8:29-30) once we choose to receive the Seed of God which is the Holy Spirit of Christ (Ephesians 1:13-14).

335} What is a biblical definition of the word Foreknow?

The biblical word Foreknow means to know before. Before what? The Father knows the future as well as He knows the past. God's foreknowledge is beyond our comprehension, but we can understand what His Word tells us in Romans 8:29. This verse is referring to an intimate knowledge. God knows us intimately as family members before the end of this life. This results in our final destination being changed to Heaven because we are identified and known as God's children. If God does not know us intimately our destiny is not Heaven (Matthew 7:23). God sees our future as clearly as if it were our present. He sees us as the new creation we will be, as if it has already happened. In God's mind, it's as good as done (Isaiah 46:9-10, Romans 4:17).

336} When did God design a plan for our salvation?

Before the foundation of the world (1-Peter 1:18-20)

337} What is a biblical definition of the word Justified?

The biblical word Justified is illustrated with the term Just-as-if-I'd-Never-Sinned. We will be completely free of all sin and shame because we will be a new creation with a new pedigree of "in Christ" instead of "in Adam." We will leave behind all association to fallen humanity just as eagles leave behind the eggshells that they were hatched from (Isaiah 40:31).

338) What is the biblical term "circumcision of the heart" a reference to?

The circumcision of the heart is referring to the removal of the fleshly human nature from our heart. Before Judgment Day, this is done by faith as we deny ourselves. Later the circumcision of the heart will be literally done as the Old Man is removed from the Children of God. At the Judgment seat of Christ our heart connection to sin will be cut off and completely removed (Colossians 2:11). The removal of the dark human spirit results in a new transformed heart (Ezekiel 36:26-27). We will have a heart of love with no room for hate. The source of corruption will be removed and replaced by the source of perfection, which is the Divine Nature of God. Our sin and even our connection to sin will be completely removed (Psalm 103:12). We will no longer be sinners. Never again will we be tempted to defile ourselves.

339) What are the three major separations (or circumcisions) coming in the future?

Separation 1: Separating the truth from the deceptions. All the darkness and gray areas will be enlightened and dispelled by the light of truth (1-Corinthians 4:5). God's Word will be proven true, wise, and forever glorified. All the lies and deceptions planted by Satan will be uprooted and exposed. Deception will never again be able to choke out the truth (Revelation 20:10). In the end everyone will know and understand "what is truth" (John 18:38).

Separation 2: Separating the saved from the lost. All those who reject God's redemption, thereby continuing in their corruption and rebellion, will be removed and quarantined in the Lake of Fire (Matthew 13:36-42, Matthew 13:47-50). They will forever be an example of the result of sin (Jude 1:7, Isaiah 66:22-24). Before Satan fell he did not realize the power and destructive ability of sin and rebellion. Adam and Eve were ignorant as well. The Lake of Fire will dispel this ignorant. Selah. The saved will experience another major separation.

Separation 3: Cutting away the Old Man, which is the identity of corruption. The fallen human nature, which produces a hard "stony heart," will be separated and removed (Ezekiel 11:19-20, Ezekiel 36:26-27). We will no longer be part of the human race, but will instead be part of the Divine family of God. The transformation will be more remarkable than when a caterpillar becomes a butterfly. Our soul will experience the refreshing removal of our core problem, the human nature (Romans 2:29, Matthew 3:10, Matthew 7:18-19). Then we will consistently act like our new identity, the children of God (Romans 8:18-19).

Further discussion questions

340} **How would you summarize this chapter?**

341} **What do you think was the most important biblical explanation to remember?**

342} **What Bible verses were the most revealing or noteworthy to you?**

343} **Can you think of ways to apply this information to your daily life?**

CHAPTER 17
THE DEVIL'S FINAL DESTINY

344} **What is the origin of evil?**

The origin of evil dates back to Satan's fall from perfection (Isaiah 14:12-15, Luke 10:18).

345} **Who was Satan at his creation?**

Satan has many names, but is most often called the Devil. In the Bible he is referred to as an "angel of light" and a fallen angel. Lucifer is also another name for Satan. The definition of Lucifer is light-bearer. God created him as a powerful good angel, an "Anointed Cherub." He was probably in charge of praise and worship to God and had radiant beauty and tremendous musical ability (Ezekiel 28:13-15).

346} What happened to Satan?

He was a powerful influence in Heaven, but he also had a mind of his own. Eventually he became proud of himself and coveted the power and position Jesus his creator rightfully possessed (Ezekiel 28:16-17). This corrupted him and made him unfit for Heaven. Therefore Satan was cast out of Heaven to this Earth (Luke 10:18, Isaiah 14:12).

347} Why does God give spiritual beings an ability to reject Him?

The ability to choose is essential to having the ability to show love. Adam and Eve could choose to obey God and remain perfect, or sin. Satan once had a choice to obey God and remain perfect or rebel. Having the ability to choose is a far more superior being than a puppet or robot. Therefore a being with a complex mind, free will and a variety of emotions has the ability for true fellowship and companionship.

348} What was the root of the first sin?

Pride (Ezekiel 28:16-17), it divided Heaven and corrupted the Earth

349} Does God categorize sins, as some being worse than others?

It's true that none of us has a position of being a self-righteous judge (Luke 18:9-14) but God does categorize sin (John 19:11) and we can agree with God. No sin is good, but some sins are more devastating to individuals and to the societies in which they live. Jesus declared that at Judgment Day some sins are considered worse than others (Matthew 11:22-24).

350} Is there a sin that that God hates more than others?

Pride is registered first in a list of sins that God hates (Proverbs 6:16-17). God considers a proud heart an abomination (Proverbs 16:5). Pride is disrespectful and can pollute our good works (Luke 18: 9-14). Pride goes before a fall (Proverbs 16:18-19). Pride creates divisions and strife (Mark 9:33-35, Mark 10:35-45). Pride was the first sin, which caused Lucifer to fall from his high position as an Anointed Cherub (Ezekiel 28:14-17, Isaiah 14:13-15). Pride is deceptive (Revelation 3:17-19).

351} What is Satan doing today?

Roaming the Earth seeking to kill, steal and destroy what God loves (1-Peter 5:8-10). The Devil is only at one place at a time but he has many demonic forces that are continually promoting evil and corruption (Ephesians 6:12).

352} Who is considered part of the first resurrection?

The "first resurrection" refers to the redeemed (both living and dead) that go to Heaven and come back to Earth with Jesus. The first resurrection are all those that are judged at the Judgment Seat of Christ and attend the Wedding Feast of the Lamb. This will include Old Testament saints and Born Again Christians. Even after the rapture of the church there are martyrs that come out of the Great Tribulation that will be part of the first resurrection (Revelation 6:9-11). All of us will receive white robes to cove our immortal bodies before the wedding feast of the Lamb (Revelation 19:6-9).

353} What is the definition of the Christian term the rapture?

Rapture means people being physically or bodily removed from the Earth.

354} The word rapture is not in the Bible, but does the Bible reveal multiple raptures?

Yes. Enoch was the first one raptured (Genesis 5:24), and then Elijah (2 Kings 2:11). The day of Jesus' resurrection, there was a "first fruits" rapture of saints who came out of their graves and gave witness to people living in Jerusalem before going to Heaven (Matthew 27:52-53), and there was Jesus' rapture (Acts 1:9). In the future there will be the rapture of the church (1-Thessalonians 4:16-17) as well as other raptures during the Great Tribulation (Revelation 11:11-12).

355} What 3 things happen to Christians after they are raptured and before they come back to Earth?

¹⁾ We will receive a new immortal body (1-Corinthians 15:51-54, 1-John 3:2).
²⁾ We will be purified and rewarded at the Judgment seat of Christ. Our lifelong activities will be judged and the Old Man (fallen human nature) will be removed. This is referred to as the circumcision of the heart (Romans 2:29). We need to have our heart circumcised so we can become perfected (Jeremiah 9:26, Acts 7:51). Having a circumcised heart is like a having a new heart with a new identity (Ezekiel 36:26-27). Then according to our good works (Romans 14:10-12) we will be given rewards and authority (Revelation 22:12).
₃⁾ We will participate in the Marriage Supper of the Lamb and be joined to God in a special way that gives us a new and completed identity as Children of God (Romans 8:18-19, Revelation 19:5-9)

₃₅₆₎ Do saints that died centuries ago have to wait hundreds of years before their soul can participate these 3 events?

Old Testament Saints had to wait for Jesus to die and set them free (Luke 16:22-23) but after Jesus' resurrection they went to Heaven, (Ephesians 4:7-10). We now live in the Church Age, which began around the time of Jesus' rapture and will end at the church's rapture. If we die during the church age we don't have to wait to go to Heaven and be with Jesus (2-Corinthians 5:8-10). The souls of the dead saints that died hundreds of years ago will go to be with Jesus as He prepares to come back to get their bodies at the rapture of the church. It is reasonable that those that die 5 minutes before the rapture of the church will appear at the same time and place as those that died 5 century's earlier. God is not limited by the flow of time. God can and has taken people form completely different times of history and brought them together to be in his presents (Matthew 17:2-5). At the rapture of the church all saints will come together (1-Thessalonians 4:13-17) and then go to face Judgment (Hebrews 9:27). Remember, God can supersede time and take people from different times and places and make them appear before Him at the same moment (Mark 9:1-7). Time will operate at a different rate in Heaven. It will seem limitless, yet orderly. We will no longer be subject to time. Time is subject to God (Joshua 10:12-14, 2-Kings 20:8-11).

357} **What global event arrives after the rapture of the church?**

The seven-year period called the Great Tribulation (Luke 21:35-36). God empowers the Church (Christ's Body) to hold back Satan's plans (2-Thessalonians 2:6-8). After the rapture of the Church, Satan will empower his final Antichrist, and tribulation will take place like the world has never known (Matthew 24:21).

358} **Does the Antichrist rule over everyone in the world?**

No, The Bible states that there are whole nations that reject him (Daniel 11:41) and suffer for it. Many people will reject the Antichrist and become saints (Revelation 13:4-8). Therefore we know the Holy Spirit is at work during the Great Tribulation because Bible mentions that there are many saints, martyrs and national revivals. They appose the Antichrist during this time (Revelation 12:17). This is why we know it is the Body of Christ not the Holy Spirit that is taken out of the way for the final Antichrist to come to power. After the church is raptured the Holy Spirit begins to open peoples eyes to what the Bibles says about the time in which they live (Revelation 7:3-4).

359} **Is the "Mark of the Beast" just a type of currency (Revelation 13:16-17), or is there something more sinister to it?**

All who receive the Mark of the Beast reject the truth about Christ and become irreversibly deceived (2-Thessalonians 2:8-12). It appears that the Mark of the Beast will be some type of computer chip that will be developed in the future that has brainwashing ability. Without exception, everyone that receives this mind-controlling chip will be deceived, reject Jesus and are doomed (Revelation 14:11, Revelation 19:20).

360} **What happens to Satan and his followers the day Jesus returns to Earth?**

Before Satan is permanently eliminated, he will be temporarily eliminated during the Millennial Reign of Christ. Satan will be removed, and Jesus will rule as King over the Earth for a thousand years (Revelation 20:1-2). The remaining nations will be judged (Matthew 25:31-33). All the people that rejected Christ and followed the Antichrist will be condemned to Hell (Matthew 25:41-46). The lost will recognize Christ's authority and call Him "Lord" before they "go away into everlasting punishment" (Philippians 2:9-11). The Antichrist and the false prophet will be judged and then be cast into the Lake of Fire (Revelation 19:20).

361} What happens to the people that rejected the Mark of the Beast and survive to see Jesus' return to Earth?

Those who resist the Antichrist and survive will repopulate the Earth, working and living their normal lives blessed by God (Matthew 25:31-34). When Jesus comes back there will be sweeping changes at every level. The human lifespan will be greatly increased (Isaiah 65:22). People will be able to live even longer than Methuselah, who died the year of the Great Flood at 969 years old. The survivors of the Great Tribulation will be similar to Noah's family because they will repopulate the Earth. They will still be mortal and will have mortal children, like Adam and Eve did.

362} Will anyone die during the millennial rein of Christ after the judgment of the nations is completed, and if so why?

Capital punishment that is sure and swift will keep most people from committing violent crimes. At 100 years old, you will still be considered a child, not that you haven't matured, but rather that you have only experienced a small portion of your potential lifespan. The only reason your life may be cut short is for crimes you commit that make you cursed and result in your execution (Isaiah 65:20). The example set forth by swift and righteous capital punishment will result in the majority of the population keeping themselves under control (Ecclesiastes 8:11). Crime will be rare, and if committed, God would bring justice quickly. Mortal people will still have their old natures. They will not be perfect. However, instead of spending time spreading corruption, they will be spending time developing their homes, enjoying their families, and enjoying the fruits of their labor (Isaiah 65:21-25).

363} Does every soul without exception have a chance to accepted Jesus as their savior?

All mankind that lived before this seventh millennium will make or have made their choice, except those who died before the age of accountability. Therefore, there are two types of people who haven't made the choice to reject Satan by personally receiving Jesus as their spiritual authority. First: Children who were born during this last millennium who multiplied and replenished the Earth. By the end of the millennium everyone, without exception, will have known Jesus for many years and will have decision-making ability. Therefore, there will be no children born near the end of this millennium (Isaiah 65:20). Second: Babies who died and people who were too mentally immature to know right from wrong. They will have developed during the millennium (2 Samuel 12:22-23) and will have the opportunity to make their personal choice. They do not get a free pass, but they will be encouraged to make the right choice.

364} What happens when this millennial rein of Christ ends?

Satan is set free to deceive in order to give the remaining members of the human race the opportunity to choose between him and Christ (Revelation 20:7-8). At the end of this last millennium Satan again denies God's Word and no doubt promises to set people free from God's rules. Because of their ignorance to the devastation of sin and rebellion, multitudes will be deceived by Satan and follow him to their destruction.

365} What does the biblical terms "as the sand of the sea" or "as the stars of heaven" signify?

They are visual references to a large number that is hard to comprehend (Judges 7:12, Hosea 1:10, Hebrews 11:12). A number we could not count to in a lifetime (Genesis 15:5).

366} Is there a final judgment day for everyone?

All those that are part of the 1st Resurrection will be judged at the Judgment seat of Christ (Romans 14:10-12, 2-Corinthians 5:10). All those not judged at the Judgment seat of Christ will be judged at the Great White Throne Judgment (Revelation 20:11-13).

367} Is everyone at the Great White Throne Judgment lost?

Everyone that was not judged at the Judgment Seat of Christ will be judged at the Great White Throne Judgment. The Judgment Seat of Christ happens before Jesus returns to rule the Earth (2-Corinthians 5:7-10, Romans 14:8-10, Revelation 20:4-6) and the Great White Throne Judgment happens after the end of the world (Revelation 20:11). There are some that come out of the Great Tribulation to repopulate the Earth. They have their names written in the book of eternal life (Revelation 13:7-8). They were not judged at the Judgment seat of Christ. Therefore, they will be judged at the Great White Throne (Revelation 20:13-15). "Whosoever" was found written in the book of life of the Lamb will enjoy Heaven for eternity. This includes these saved mortals that come out of the Great Tribulation and enter the last millennium. They will die by the end of the last rebellion, but they will not go to Hell because their names are written in the Lamb's Book of Eternal Life. All those that died throughout all the ages that are not in the Lamb's Book of Life, end up going to Hell to await their judgment (Hebrews 9:27). All those in Hell will be judged at the Great White Throne Judgment. Revelation 20:13 states that some that died and stand at the Great White Throne Judgment did not come from Hell. Revelation 20:13 states there are 3 places that those to be judged will come from. Some came from their place of death; some of them died in the sea and went directly to this judgment, instead of going to Hell. The phrase **"the sea gave up the dead which were in it;"** *reveals that these people died after the Jesus' return (Revelation 19:11-16, Jude 1:14-15, Matthew 25:31-34, Matthew 25:41) and before the end of the world, because there was still a sea (Revelations 21:1). The word "death" represents those that had their names in the Lamb's book of Life and died in the last rebellion that results in the end of the world. They will be judged, not condemned at the Great White Throne Judgment. Therefore, the simple answer to the question is, almost everyone, but not everyone is lost at this last judgment.*

368) Is the Lake of Fire a real place, and if so, is it eternal?

The Bible emphasizes that the Lake of Fire will last forever and EVER (Revelation 20:10, Revelation 14:11, Matthew 25:46). The Bible is clear that neither Satan nor anyone else ever comes out of the Lake of Fire.

369) Does Heaven have a graveyard, and if so, why?

The Bible often mentions the 2nd death (Revelation 20:6,14). There is a place (a graveyard) that God has designated and set apart to contain the dead. Sad to say, before sin no such place was needed (Matthew 25:41) but it will be a memorial revealing that death is the result of sin (James 1:15). We will not cease to exist. Our spirits are immortal and will continue "for ever and ever." If our soul did not last forever, there would be no need for an eternal destination for the lost. They would just leave a legacy and then disintegrate. Since spirits are eternal, they need an eternal destination. The Bible states that after Judgment Day there are only two destinations for an immortal spirit – Heaven or the Lake of Fire (Revelation 20:10-15). Angels are also immortal spirits (Jude 1:6). Judgment day will reveal the restricted destiny for both fallen humanity and fallen angels (Revelation 20:10). The Lake of Fire is not for redemption; it is a necessity to quarantine the satanic and rebellious from corrupting the godly. God will not allow corruption to take over Heaven as it has the Earth. The Earth is an example of what happens to a perfect world after a small seed of corruption is planted and allowed to grow. There will never be a need for future creations to experiment with corruption or rebellion, because they can see a complete history lesson at the Lake of Fire (Jude 1:7). Nothing will be hidden. There will be no mystery. All of the knowledge of good and evil will be revealed (1-Corinthians 10:5-11). Instead of deception, there will be perception. It will be obvious how a seed of sin can grow and destroy a perfect world, resulting in endless suffering. This will allow everyone to make an undeceived and wise choice to obey our loving Creator and remain perfect, rather than being ushered into the world of corruption (Hebrews 10:26-27, Hebrews 6:4-6, Isaiah 66:24, Hebrews 12:1). The coming Great Tribulation will never be repeated (Matthew 24:21) because all of Heaven will be aware of the Lake of Fire and what it contains and how it came to be. We will be perfected free moral agents and retain our free will to choose God's ways or rebel. Nevertheless, no one will be tempted lose their perfection and join that satanic rebellion or start their own.

370) How would you describe the three different sections of the book of Revelation?

1) *The church age is addressed in Revelation chapters 1 through 3. Then John is caught up to Heaven and God gives him a variety of spiritual visions.*

2) *In chapters 4 through 19, there is a lot of symbolism mixed in with John's literal observations. I believe that in these chapters the Bible reveals several points of view on at least three subjects: the Great Tribulation, Jesus and Satan's activities, and the end of ungodly government. However, they are not necessarily in order. Whenever you read something along the lines of "and I saw," "and I beheld" or "after this I beheld," it is beginning a new point of view. If you read the center section of the book of Revelation with this in mind instead of trying to put everything together chronologically it will make more sense.*

3) *Chapter 19 is a transitional chapter. It contains a lot of symbolism but it also begins the chronological portion of the book. Revelation 19 through 22 describes the progression from this creation to God's next grand creation and reveals our future home.*

Further discussion questions

371} **How would you summarize this chapter?**

372} **What do you think was the most important biblical explanation to remember?**

373} **What Bible verses were the most revealing or noteworthy to you?**

374} **Can you think of ways to apply this information to your daily life?**

CHAPTER 18
HEAVEN

375} **Describe the 3 Heavens.**

The first heaven is our atmosphere around the Earth, our sky where the clouds drift by and the birds fly (Genesis 1:20). The second heaven is the great outer space, full of darkness, dotted with countless stars (Genesis 1:14-18). The first heaven surrounds the Earth, and the second heaven surrounds the first heaven. The third Heaven, where God was when He created the first two heavens (Genesis 1:1), surrounds outer space (the second heaven). The third Heaven has a Capital City where the throne of God is located. The third Heaven surrounds the first two heavens physically as well as spiritually. By spiritually, I am talking about dimensions beyond our three-dimensional universe.

376} Is Earth an eternal part of Heaven?

Yes, the Earth will be a part of Heaven (Revelation 21:1). The Earth as we know it will be destroyed. The last time Earth was destroyed was during Noah's Great Flood. There was a transparent h2o layer in the atmosphere (the first heaven) to shield the people from the harmful radiation of the sun. It was a much better filter than our present ozone layer. The Earth was like a greenhouse, and people lived longer in a healthier environment. The water surrounding the Earth came down, and the floods came up from under the ground (earth). The world we know now is much different than the world before Noah's flood (2-Peter 3:5-7). The Earth will be completely renovated by fire, removing all contamination and then remade (Ecclesiastes 1:4). The cleansing renovation by water was minor compared to the destruction and purifying renovation that is coming by fire (Hebrews 1:10-12).

377} What is "the Day of the Lord" a reference to?

Following the Great Tribulation there is an initial wave of judgment upon Jesus' return to Earth (Revelation 19:15), followed by a period of peace (Isaiah 11:4-9). This is the "Day of the Lord" which will last a thousand years (2-Peter 3:8). Jesus will judge and govern this Earth for a thousand years (Revelation 20:6). The many references to the "Day of the Lord" focus on the beginning judgment and the concluding Great White Throne Judgment (Revelation 20:11). In the final wave of judgment, we see heaven and Earth departing (Revelation 6:14-17, Revelation 20:11-12). The Day of the Lord refers to Jesus ruling as King of the Earth for a thousand years, but that is like the first day of an eternal kingdom, because Jesus' kingdom has no end (Daniel 2:44).

378} In Heaven, will our sins be remembered against us?

The Old Man has deceived me at times and contaminated my life, but I am not the Old Man. I am a "new creature" (2-Corinthian 5:17). You are a "new creature" in Christ if you have asked Jesus's Spirit into your heart. Sin will not be identified with us, because it and everything attached to the Old Man will be permanently separated from us (Psalm 103:12) on judgment day. We will truly be a new creation in Christ (Romans 8:1). We are born-again into a new family with a new heritage. We will no longer be sinners associated with shame, but instead we will be seen as stars in the family of God (Daniel 12:3). When we are glorified, no shame or hint of darkness will linger. We will be perfected and surrounded by the Joy of the Lord.

379) What are the measurements of the capital city in Heaven?

The bottom of the first foundation would be about 1400 to 1500 miles long and 1400 to 1500 miles wide. The city is also 1400 to 1500 miles tall (Revelation 21:16).

380) How many foundations does the New Jerusalem have?

The walls have 12 foundations (Revelation 21:14), not piled on top of one another, which would be one foundation comprised of 12 materials. It would make a lot of sense that if you had a 1500-mile-tall city, there would be levels or, in this case, 12 floors or foundations. There could be more than 100 miles between one floor and the next level up. That's higher than our atmosphere, our first heaven.

381) Why is a Jasper stone a good way to visualize the New Jerusalem?

The walls and the bottom floor will look like jasper that is "clear as crystal." Jasper is not naturally clear and is hard to describe exactly because it can be found in any and every color, including black and white. It is often multiple colors with differing designs or patterns. Jasper can appear spotted or have a linear pattern. On one side, a jasper stone can look like a beautiful sunset over a mountain range, while the other side might be completely different. This is why jasper is such a good gem to describe the exterior of the Capital City. The sidewalls of the city will no doubt have lines where the 12 foundations (levels) connect or protrude as balconies. The bottom would be more spotted with an array of shapes, lines, and colors because of the roads, rivers, landscapes, and mansions above it. The base and the walls are transparent, "clear as crystal" and "like unto clear glass," similar to a diamond. However, unlike a diamond, there will be a collage of colors and patterns under the surface resembling a polished jasper stone.

382) Does the New Jerusalem have pearly gates and if so how many?

Yes, there are gates in the capital city of Heaven (Revelation 22:14). There are 12 pearly gates (Revelation 21:12,21) and four walls. Each wall has three gates or entrances (Revelation 21:13). Because of the walls thickness these entrances will be like tunnels (Revelation 21:17). Because there are 12 floors each floor would have 1 entrance gate, just as there is 1 door to enter Heaven (John 10:9).

383) Will the capital city of Heaven be located on the new Earth?

We don't know the size of the new Earth, but the New Jerusalem is 1400-1500 miles tall, so it would probably throw a planet out of balance if it sat on it. Also, the larger the planet is, the larger the shadow of obscurity would be. The light from the city needs to be above the planet just to illuminate ½ of it. The planet and or the city would also need to have an orbit in order for the light to shine on the whole Earth at some point. The New Jerusalem descends to the new Earth (Revelation 21:1-3) but positions itself above the Earth like a satellite city. The light of the New Jerusalem shines down to illuminate the new Earth like the sun and moon do now (Revelation 21:23-24).

384) Will we have physical bodies in Heaven?

Our eternal bodies will be amazing. They will be tangible, not like a ghost. Our heavenly bodies will be touchable, like Christ's body after His resurrection (Philippians 3:21, Luke 24:36-40). The Bible gives us a few hints of the abilities of the glorious resurrection body. In our resurrection body we can enjoy food and drink (Luke 24:41-42, Matthew 26:29). Our supernatural bodies will have the same ability as Jesus and the angels. Like the *angels, our new bodies will have powers and abilities far beyond anything in this world. Just like Jesus, we will be able to travel unlimited distances and it will be no harder than the simple decision to make the trip.*

385) Does every Christian have a beautiful mansion in Heaven?

God is the one who prepares our mansion and location in His house (John 14:2). There will be no homeless people in Heaven. Everyone will have their own beautiful home in Paradise as a gift, specially prepared for them by Jesus their King. Everyone's mansion will be glorious because Jesus paid the price to give us our dream homes. We can't earn our heavenly place. We will not compete with each other for our place in this capital city. I'm not trying to take your place and trying to take my place won't fulfill or benefit you. There are simply no bad neighborhoods or shabby shacks in Heaven (Matthew 20:1-15).

386) In Heaven does everyone have the same wealth or are some richer than others?

Some lay up treasures in Heaven and accumulate eternal wealth and some do not (Matthew 6:20). Therefore, some have much more wealth than others. Some have homes that are much better furnished than others and they have vehicles to enjoy all that heaven has to offer. Jesus paid for our heavenly home and gave it to us as a free gift, but Jesus also gives us opportunities to fill our homes with treasures by doing good works. Jesus also gives us opportunities to qualify to have authority over larger territories outside of God's capital city (Luke 19:10-26). It is our treasurers and abilities in heaven that we work for, not our home in heaven.

387) Are there animals in Heaven?

God likes variety. Horses are one of the many animals in Heaven (Revelation 19:11). We can have our own horses to ride (Revelation 19:14). Everything in Heaven will be better than what we experience in this life, including love for animals and their love for us (1-Corinthians 13:13). Many animals are mentioned in describing the millennial reign of Christ (Isaiah 11:6-9) and therefore included in God's eternal kingdom (Daniel 2:44). In Heaven the animals will not kill or be violent (Isaiah 65:25). They will have improved bodies with improved digestive systems. In Heaven all the good elements of this life will be enhanced.

388) Will we have memories of people and events of this life in Heaven?

The Bible is an eternal book and can be read in Heaven. It contains history and the process of redemption. It also states that nothing will be hidden (Luke 8:17, Luke 12:2). Therefore, we will know our friends as well as people that we read about in the Bible (1-Corinthians 13:12). We will also understand history and spiritual influences better than ever before. We will see and talk with Jesus about many things regarding this life and He will answer all our questions.

389) Is the millennial reign of Christ similar to what Heaven will be like in eternity?

The millennial reign of Christ is the beginning of Jesus' eternal kingdom on Earth. This same kingdom will not end at the end of the millennium, but instead will continue forever (Daniel 2:44). The Millennial Reign of Christ may reflect what Heaven is like more than we realize. One of the things we see in the Millennial Reign of Christ is that there are 2 types of people on Earth. There are the survivors of the Great Tribulation (Matthew 25:31-34) and members of the 1st resurrection (Revelation 20:4-6). The survivors of the Great Tribulation are not part of the 1st resurrection. To be part of the first resurrection you need to be raptured or died before the Judgment Seat of Christ (2-Corinthians 5:10) and the Wedding Feast of the Lamb (Revelation 19:7-8). At the Judgment Seat of Christ we are made ready for the Wedding. We will receive rewards for good works (1-Corinthians 3:13-15). We will also be set free from our sinful human nature which the Bible refers to as the Old Man (Matthew 22:8-13). It is our soul not our human nature that is covered with the robe of righteousness (Isaiah 61:10 KJV). After we have been delivered from our fallen sinful human nature and received our rewards then at the wedding we are joined to Christ as a new creation. Because we retain the Nature of God, we can truly become a part of the family of God (Romans 8:18-23). Once the judgment and wedding has concluded there will be no more additions to the first resurrection (Revelation 20:6). All this takes place before

Jesus comes back to Earth to rule and rein (Revelation 19:11-14). When Jesus comes back to Earth only those that have their names in the book of eternal life (Revelation 13:7-8) will be able to enter and repopulate this kingdom of God on Earth (Isaiah 11:4, Isaiah 65:20-23). They will have an eternal home in paradise as the nations of the redeemed (Revelation 21:24). The difference between the millennial reign of Christ and Heaven is that in Heaven there will be absolutely no sin because nobody in Heaven has a sinful nature. Also, in Heaven there is no corruption or waste, but instead eternal perfection is everywhere (Matthew 5:48, Revelation 21:27). The new Earth, which is contained in the new Heaven, is eternally beautiful. God's capital city is eternally glorious and shines down on the new Earth as the sun does now (Revelation 21:22-26).

390} What are the characteristics of those that are the in leadership positions in Heaven?

In Heaven, the leadership does not rule over others as kings do now. It's more like a respectful and considerate family. Loving parents are in charge and take care of the children. The greatest in Heaven will be those who have the greatest ability to serve and will love doing so. The least in Heaven will have the least ability to serve (Matthew 20:25-28).

391} Will there be time in Heaven and if so how is time different in eternity?

There is a progression of time and development in Heaven (Revelation 21:1-5), as well as specific times for special events (Revelation 19:7). Time will operate at a different rate in Heaven. It will seem limitless, yet orderly. We will no longer be subject to time. Instead, time will be subject to us, the family of God (Joshua 10:12-14, 2-Kings 20:8-11).

392} Will there be celebrations and reunions in Heaven that include eating and drinking?

There will be small (Genesis 49:33) and large (Revelation 19:1) gatherings in Heaven. There will be special times of celebration as well as eating and drinking in Heaven (Matthew 26:29, Exodus 12:17, Revelation 19:9).

393} Are out-of-body experiences real, and if so are they a reliable account of life after death?

As mentioned in chapter 1 of Deep Foundations, we always need to test the spirits to see the source of the information (1-John 4:1). The tool for this test is God's Word, the Bible. In the Bible there were some that had Temporary out-of-body experiences (Revelation 4:1-2). Ezekiel describes an out-of-body experience in Ezekiel 11:1-2. I believe Jesus had an out-of-body experience as part of Satan's temptations (Matthew 4:8). Paul mentions an out-of-body experience in 2-Corinthians 12:2-4. Like in the Bible some saints may get a glimpse of Judgment Day, some part of Heaven, the millennial reign of Christ or even or Hell. These experiences can help us visualize what the Bible states on these subjects but do not replace the Word of God. If a vision contradicts the Word of God then it cannot be trusted. Temporary euphoric out-of-body experiences can be a deceptive temptation from the Devil (Luke 4:5-8) to make you think you don't need to follow God's Word to enter glory. Satan, the angel of light can seduce some individuals with a temporary heavenly experience through drugs or death (temporarily clinically dead), but only God can give you eternal life in Heaven. Those preaching or believing in a false gospel will not be blessed by God in the end. The gospel is God's plan for salvation. It tells us how to receive eternal life, which qualifies us for Heaven. If a nonbeliever has a temporary vision of the light of God or life in paradise and then they are revived, they may become a believer and receive salvation. Although, if a nonbeliever has a temporary vision of the light of God or life in paradise and they think they will get to Heaven without being "born-again" then they have been deceived by the Devil. Satan may use them and their temporary experience to mislead others into thinking everyone will spend eternity in Heaven or that their experience trumps the Bible. It doesn't matter how real a mirage may seem, it will evaporate on Judgment Day when all deceptions are removed and we clearly see the truth.

Further discussion questions

394} How would you summarize this chapter?

395} What do you think was the most important biblical explanation to remember?

396} What Bible verses were the most revealing or noteworthy to you?

397} Can you think of ways to apply this information to your daily life?

CHAPTER 19
RECONCILING APPARENT CONTRADICTIONS

398} Are there errors in the Word of God?

There are mistranslations, misinterpretations and verses that are hard to reconcile but there are no mistakes in the Word of God (2-Timothy 3:16-17, 1-Peter 1:23-25).

399} Where do we find to the keys to understand the mysteries and the doctrines of the Bible?

The Bible contains within itself the interpretation of its symbolism and concepts (Isaiah 28:9-10, 2-Peter 1:20-21, 2-Timothy 2:15). That is why we need to gather all the passages on the subject to properly establish well-balanced biblical doctrines. Unbiblical religious doctrines bring confusion, blindness and even satanic bondage. Well-balanced biblical doctrines bring illumination and wisdom to make better decisions resulting in freedom to enjoy a fulfilling endless life (John 8:32).

400} What type of book is extremely helpful in doing word searches in the Bible?

An Exhaustive Concordance that contains every word found in the Bible as well as Greek and Hebrew word definitions.

401} Who is the final authority on what the Word of God is saying?

Although it is good to study and do word searches of the Bible, it is the Holy Spirit that will put the Bible in the proper perspective so we can see the truth clearly (John 14:16-17). The Holy Spirit accurately teaches us the deep and complex things from God (John 14:26). The Holy Spirit of God is the final authority for proper interpretation of the Bible (John 16:13-15). The Holy Spirit will never contradict or be inconsistent with the written Word of God. It is easy to become inconsistent in our doctrines and religious beliefs if we resist the Holy Spirit's correction and direction (1-Corinthians 2:12-14). The Holy Spirit will often use others to teach us. However, we need to continue to discern when the Holy Spirit is using them. We do this by continually using the Word of God to verify the Spirit of Truth (1-John 4:1).

402} How does the old story of three blind men describing an elephant apply to conflicting doctrines?

First let's review of the story: One blind man is at the foot and claims an elephant is firm like an oak tree. Another is at the tail and says no an elephant is flexible like a rope. The third blind man is at the head and says you are both wrong it is Simi-rigid like a large water hose. Who is right and who is wrong? Everyone is right about describing what they are felling, but they are all wrong about describing an elephant. What we feel can lead us astray. It is easy to get confused if you don't see the big picture. We need to have faith in the God's Word, not faith in our feelings or presumptions. The problem with teaching things that is inconsistent with the big picture, is that it causes distortion and confusion. Biblical confusion results in unbalanced church doctrines, which divide the body of Christ. We are free to have diversity in style (Luke 9:49-50) but we should be unified in truth (John 17:17-21).

403} What should we do with Bible verses and concepts that we do not understand?

Things we do not understand should not sidetrack us, but instead help us to realize there are things the Holy Spirit has yet to reveal to us (John 16:12-13). We should primarily focus on connecting to the Holy Spirit and consider what God is clearly showing us. By reflecting on what God has shown us, the Holy Spirit will illuminate our next step and expand our comprehension of our situation. However, we should not completely ignore puzzling Bible verses because they may be the key to our greatest revelations. The best thing to do with puzzling passages is to keep them in our heart and pray for wisdom to see how they fit the big biblical picture (Psalm 119:18).

404} What is the proper explanation of Mark 16:16, which is in harmony with the whole Bible?

There are three points to understand and connect in order to see what is actually stated in Mark 16:16.

<u>First:</u> A clue for proper interpretation is actually contained in the verse itself. The verse concludes with, "He that believeth not shall be damned." Therefore, the damned are all those who do not believe.

<u>Second:</u> The Bible teaches that water baptism is not necessary for salvation (John 3:16, John 6:47, Romans 10:13). Mark began his gospel by quoting John the Baptist who was pointing out there is a Spiritual baptism (Mark 1:8).

<u>Third:</u> Mark 16:16 actually confirms the doctrine of salvation, that you must first believe in Jesus' atoning work on the cross and then receive the baptism of Holy Spirit as your spiritual covering and soul mate. It is the Holy Spirit that immerses us into the spiritual body of Christ (1-Corinthians 12:12-14). It is because of the Holy Spirit that you are born-again into the family of God and have a home in Heaven. Simply put, you first need to believe and then receive Jesus' Spirit into your heart, thus beginning the eternal relationship between you and God (Romans 8:9-23).

405} What is the reason for being baptized in water?

True Christian water baptism happens after we are born again. It is an action of obedience and discipleship. Baptism is a choice we make to yield to Jesus as Lord of our lives after we have received him as Savior of our souls. Baptism is a meaningful and glorious ceremony we go through to identify with the death, burial, and resurrection of Jesus. Thus, going beneath the water and rising out of it is a symbol and testimony of our death and burial to self in order to enjoy our resurrection life in Christ (Romans 6:3-4).

406} According to the Bible, what is essential for us to do to qualify for Heaven?

Receive the Holy Spirit in our heart is the only thing we need for our salvation (Romans 8:14-15, Romans 8:9, John 14:16). It is the Holy Spirit that transforms us into children of God, not water-baptism or good works.

407} How can our salvation experience be compared to a baseball game?

Believing is like getting on base. It doesn't matter if you are on first, second, or third base, you need to get to home-plate (receive the Holy Spirit of Jesus) before the inning is over, to make it count on the scoreboard. It is after we believe: $^{1st\ base}$ God is the creator, $^{2nd\ base}$ Jesus is God and became a sinless man, $^{3rd\ base}$ Jesus died for my sins and offers me salvation as a free gift, then I can $^{get\ to\ home-plate}$ receive salvation and make it count. It is after I believe and receive Jesus' Holy Spirit into my heart that I can be properly water baptized to celebrate and demonstrate my dedication to Jesus.

408} Can we stop God from doing what He wants to do?

Yes. Although no one can stop God's grand plan for establishing His Kingdom on Earth, we can limit God from using us. By skepticism, ignorance and disobedient we stop God from fulfilling His desire to bless us (Matthew 13:58, Acts 7:51, 2-Chronicles 30:8-9, 2-Peter 3:9).

409} Is breaking the fourth Commandment, regarding the weekly Sabbath always considered a sin?

Jesus never sinned, yet He was called a Sabbath breaker (John 5:16-18, John 9:16). The Sabbath was established for our good, because we need to set aside a day for rest and reflection (Mark 2:27). The Law provides an exception to this commandment for the priests of the temple (Matthew 12:5, Hebrews 4:14). If we are in Christ we are free from the law and are considered priest (Romans 12:5, Romans 8:1-2, Colossians 2:16, 1-Peter 2:9).

410} Why do most Christian churches assemble on 1st day of the week (Sunday) instead of the last day (Saturday)?

Since we are legally free, it is good for us to gather on Sundays to worship God. Sunday is a unique day of the week with special significance to our redemption. *Sunday is the day of Jesus Christ's Resurrection. The first disciples came together on Sunday and seen Jesus in their midst (John 20:19). Sunday is the same day as the first fruits wave offering according to Leviticus 23:10-12. There were special events in the Jewish year that only happened on Sunday. Starting at this first fruits Sunday as day one, the 50th day was the Sunday of Pentecost (which the Jews call the Feast of Weeks) Leviticus 23:15-16. It was the day the Holy Spirit empowered the disciples for evangelism (Acts 2:1-8). Pentecost was on Sunday, the day "after the seventh Sabbath," the "first day of the week." Sunday is a spiritually significant day for the followers of Christ. You could say the birth of the church happened on Sunday. Sunday remained a day for first fruits offerings and for collections to help the saints in need (1-Corinthians 16:1-2). Christians gathered on Sundays to celebrate the rising of the Son, not the sun. The reason the early disciples habitually gathered on Resurrection Day was to praise God and remember Jesus with the Lord's Supper. They also honored God's Word and examined ways to apply it (Acts 20:7). Sunday was a special day that the early disciples came together to encourage each other and gave offerings. We should continue to do the same. Any day people come together to do these things is a good day.*

411} **What is the potentially blameless spirit that is listed with our soul and body in 1-Thessalonians 5:23?**

It is the unseen motivator of the heart not the human nature.

412} **What is the parallel verse to 1-Thessalonians 5:23?**

*Deuteronomy 6:5: **And thou shalt love the LORD thy God with all thine <u>heart</u>, and with all thy <u>soul</u>, and with all thy <u>might</u>.***

413} **What is the three-fold cord of devotion and how does it work, according to the book Deep Foundations?**

The three parts that we can unify with God is, our heart, our soul, and our body. This three-fold cord of devotion starts with the heart illuminating the soul and finally leads to the body's actions of love, devotion and sacrifice.

414} **Is the Divine Nature always good?**

Yes

415} In God's eyes, is the fallen human nature always bad?

Yes

416} How does refueling our car symbolize elements of our spiritual life?

The fuel represents the Divine nature or the human nature. The hose represents our heart. The heart is not the fuel, but it can transfer the fuel of our choice and refuel our car, or spiritually speaking, reenergize our soul's attitudes and body's actions. We can be naturally motivated, but we can also choose to circumcise the connection to the Old Man, refocus on our relationship with God and change our motivation. Love should be our primary motivator. Love is key indicator that the Holy Spirit of God is in control of us and that we have His identity. Love is the main fruit of the Holy Spirit. Without love, the gifts of the Spirit become contaminated and will not operate correctly. Love is like the fuel that propels a car to its destination. If we are low on fuel, we have a choice – either fill up or fall short. Even if I have the most beautiful, powerful, expensive auto of my dreams, it will leave me stranded and be of little use if I don't continually refuel. God gives us the spiritual gifts and talents (our vehicle). However, it is up to us to keep our vehicle clean and refueled for service.

417} Does our soul have a choice to receive or reject the thought seed coming out of our heart?

All kinds of thoughts will come out of our heart but our soul has a choice to receive or reject the thought seeds. If we receive consistent seed it will eventually bear fruit and come through our soul in the form of expressed ideas, actions, and attitudes. Sometimes it takes just one seed to significantly change our perception of a situation. We will be held accountable for what we permit to cross the heart bridge and bear fruit in our soul. That is why we need to guard our heart and not let bitterness, or any form of ungodliness take root in our heart (Proverbs 4:23). We have one heart but many times it is compartmentalized into different cambers of information. A divided heart is like having two hearts that are contrary to each other. God sees the different counsels that inspire and influence our actions as being connected to one of two types of hearts. One heart-chamber speaks with the selfish wisdom of this world and is in unity with the Deceiver himself. The other heart-chamber is connected to the heavenly Counselor, offering eternal wisdom rooted in love. We hear both of these counsels. The question is, which one do we plug into and consider, thereby receiving inspiration and motivation? It is our choice.

418} What 3 arias will we be judged in?

The three categories God is looking at on judgment day are our motives (Matthew 6:1-6), our attitudes (2-Corinthians 9:7), and our actions (1-Corinthians 3:14). Our motives are as important as our attitudes and actions in determining whether we will be held blameless and receive praise and rewards (1-Corinthians 4:5).

419} Why is a good explanation of a puzzling verse not always a good thing?

We need to be cautious that an explanation is not actually a rationalization. That is why even with a good explanation of a puzzling verse, it's still important to find a second witness or a back-up verse that states the same or similar thing (Isaiah 28:9-10). The Bible calls for two or three witnesses to establish a matter (2-Corinthians 13:1). With the proper perspective and correct interpretation, there are no contradictions within the God's Word.

420} Why does the Bible often refer to God as the light?

The light drives out darkness and illuminates our situation (1-John 1:5-6, John 12:35). The light allows us to see things more clearly, but many do not want the truth to be exposed (John 3:19-21, Ephesians 5:12-14). There is a revealing contrast between God's kingdom of light and Satan's realm of darkness.

421} Will it change anything in our dark world, if it sees the light of truth?

There are many that are discouraged and tired of the direction this world has been going. They are ready for revival (John 4:35). There are others that are blinded by deception just as Saul (Paul) was, but if they see the light and comprehend the truth they would be transformed. Jesus is the truth (John 14:6) and the light of the world (John 8:12, John 9:5) and when He went to Heaven He commissioned His body (Christians) to continue His work and reflect the light of truth to the world (Ephesians 5:8, Matthew 5:14-16, Acts 26:18).

422) **What enables Satan to blind people and keep them in darkness?**

If people that are entrusted with the light do not share it (Ezekiel 33:8, Luke 11:23), but instead hide it (Luke 8:16), then darkness will prevail (Proverbs 4:19). Satan wants to hide and divide us, so he can continue to deceive and corrupt our communities. The Deceiver wants us to fear correcting commonly accepted heresies. Satan wants us to promote our unbiblical traditions and conflicting doctrines instead of the truth (Isaiah 5:20-23, Matthew 23:24, 2-Corinthians 11:13-15, Titus 3:3, 1-Timothy 1:13). Satan also wants us to pass his distortions of the truth onto the new believers as well as the next generation (1-Timothy 4:1, 2-Timothy 4:3-4, 2-Timothy 3:13, Acts 17:30).

423) **To not know I am deceived is considered to be** _ignorant_, **but if I know the truth and reject it is considered** _rebellion_.

424) **What is God's warning to religious people that aid Satan in spreading his distortions and lies?**

Colossians 2:8 *"Beware lest any man spoil you through philosophy and vain deceit, after the tradition of men, after the rudiments of the world, and not after Christ."* **Mark 7:7ᵦ-8ₐ** *"In vain do they worship me, teaching for doctrines the commandments of men. For laying aside the commandment of God, ye hold the tradition of men."* **Mark 7:9** *"And he said unto them, Full well ye reject the commandment of God, that ye may keep your own tradition."* **Mark 7:13** *"Making the word of God of none effect through your tradition, which ye have delivered: and many such like things do ye."* **Matthew 15:13-14** *"He answered and said, every plant, which My heavenly Father hath not planted, shall be rooted up. Let them alone: they be blind leaders of* *the blind. And if the blind lead the blind, both shall fall into the ditch."*

425} **Are there many people (including Christens) that are skeptical of the Bible, and if so, why?**

Yes, many people including Christens are skeptical of the Bible. There are many religious leaders that doubt Jesus' own words. For example, Matthew 12:40 plainly states that Jesus would be in the tomb 3 days and 3 nights. The book Deep Foundations reveals the accuracy of that biblical statement. Yet there are many that believe Jesus died at the end of Friday and rose early Sunday. This conflict with Jesus' words in the Bible promotes confusion and skepticism. Satan would have us doubt the meticulous precision of God's Word. The Deceiver wants us to replace wisdom with blind faith in something that doesn't add up. This rejection of God's Word promotes gullibility and blindness. It makes people vulnerable to blindly accept other deceptions, such as saying things like the Bible is subject to many interpretations and there is no absolute truth. In reality God's Word is not subject to our opinion, which would make our opinion the final authority (2-Peter 1:20-21, 2-Timothy 3:16-17). The wise will have their opinion subject to God's Word, which is the final authority at judgment day. There are some errors in the translations of the Bible which is pointed out in question 185. Even though some translators have made mistakes and Satan attempts to counterfeit and distort the truth of God's Word (2-Corinthians 2:17, 2-Corinthians 4:2), there is no mistake in God's Original Word. God's Word is eternal, incorruptible, and indestructible (1-Peter 1:23-25). It is wise to learn, trust and apply God's Word as a foundation to all we do (Matthew 7:24-28).

426} **Do I have to lose my individuality to unify with the body of Christ?**

No, God does not what you to lose your uniqueness and be a clone of someone else. God wants us to unify and become one in revealing the Light of Truth. This does not mean we lose our individuality (1-Corinthians 12:4-31). God does not want us to become hypocrites just ignorantly parroting each other. Instead, God wants us to walk in truth. God wants us to fulfill our special purpose and grow so that we would be more influential to expand God's kingdom and enjoy more consistently producing the fruit of the Spirit.

427) When and where did Jesus pray that all His followers would be united in truth?

Near the end of Jesus' mortal life He prayed that we would be one in the truth. Jesus' prayer to the Father about the church being unified in truth is found in John 17:17-23.

428) Has Jesus' prayer about the church being unified in the truth been fulfilled yet?

Maybe at the birth of the church (Acts 2:41-47). But the Bible reveals that the early church had divisions between Hebrews and Greeks (Acts 6:1) with debates over food, customs and circumcision (Acts 15:1-10, Galatians 2:1-14). In Paul's time there were not only divisions between the Jewish and Gentile church, but there were also many divisions within the Gentile church (1-Corinthians 3:2-4). If we look at the church in 2020 there are still many divisions with many conflicting doctrines that misrepresent the Bible. For instance, there is still confusion and controversy, even in the most basic and important doctrine, which is what it takes to be saved. One church claims you need to be baptized in water to be saved, another claims you need to stop sinning and be good to be saved, and yet another claims that God chooses who will be saved and who will be lost. There are also churches that proclaim we only need to ask the Spirit of Jesus into our heart to be saved. Someday Jesus' prayer will be answered and the body of Christ will come together and unify in biblical truth (Ephesians 4:13-16). Then the world will see the beauty and glory of the unified Body of Christ truly reflecting God and His Word (John 17:22-23).

429) Is there time for another Great Awakening?

Yes, if you understood chapter 6 of the book Deep Foundations you know we have plenty of time for revivals and even another Great Awakening before the end of the world. The question is, will Jesus' prayer in John 17:17-23 be answered in our generation, or will Jesus have to wait.

430} **If there were another Great Awakening, what do you think its main thrust and legacy would be?**

This is the information age. Finding eternal truth in a sea of conflicting information can be difficult. I believe the foundation and legacy of the next Great Awakening is unity in biblical truth. This would be an answer to Jesus' heart felt prayer for the church found in John 17:17-23.

431} **What kind of church is Jesus coming back for?**

There may be some defeated Christians that will be raptured, but Jesus is not coming back for an oppressed, lukewarm church that needs to be rescued from this world. Jesus is coming back for His bride who has made herself ready (Revelation 19:7) by being washed in the water of God's Word (Ephesians 5:26). By God's Word and with God's Spirit the spots of darkness will be cleansed and the wrinkles of unbiblical doctrines will be ironed out (Ephesians 5:27). The church Jesus is coming back for has a reputation of keeping God's Word in spite of conflict (Revelation 3:8-10). Jesus is coming back for a wise church that truly knows Him personally and is prepared and proclaiming the light of truth (Matthew 25:1-13, Matthew 5:14-16).

Further discussion questions

432} **How would you summarize this chapter?**

433} **What do you think was the most important biblical explanation to remember?**

434} **What Bible verses were the most revealing or noteworthy to you?**

435} **Can you think of ways to apply this information to your daily life?**

www.ingramcontent.com/pod-product-compliance
Lightning Source LLC
Chambersburg PA
CBHW060804050426
42449CB00008B/1534